Practical Awareness of Living in the Presence of God

You will show me the way of life, granting me the joy of your presence and the pleasures of living with you forever. Psalm 16:11 (NLT)

James Perry

Practical Awareness of Living in the Presence of God

ISBN 9780984570881

A Dedication

Psalm 127:3 states, "Behold, children are a heritage from the Lord, the fruit of the womb a reward."

Psalm 128:3 states: "Your wife will be like a fruitful vine within your house; your children will be like olive shoots around your table."

When one is called to be a Pastor, it often entails relocation from time to time. This is especially true when one is willing to serve the smaller congregations – some of them with fifty of fewer people.

Our commitment to serve the Lord was a willingness to go anywhere, at any time, to do any work, at any cost. It became an emotional time – especially for our children – when the time for moving to a new location came.

One day, as the Father of four children, I sat them down and apologized to them for the relocations, changing schools, having to make new friends, etc. My eldest daughter, who became the self-appointed spokesperson for the children responded: "But Dad, small churches need good Pastors too." Those words have meant much during the years of serving the Lord.

It is with joy that this book is dedicated to my four children: Beth, Andy, Martha, and Becca. In different ways, they are a real part of the ministry journey and accomplishment. Their Mother was able to guide them well - and for her and them, I am grateful.

Foreword

When One spends time in the Holy Scriptures and meditates upon God's Word, it becomes very apparent how awesome God is and how unworthy mankind is to even think one has a right to approach Him

The use of Psalms, Hymns and Spiritual Songs is also a source to sharpen one's focus and worship. One of the Contemporary Choruses that fits this discussion of walking and living in the presence of God, as well as a worship time with Him is:

Holy Lord, most Holy Lord. You alone are worthy of my praise Oh Holy Lord, most Holy Lord With all of my heart I sing – Great are you, Lord – Worthy of Praise, Holy and True – Great are you Lord, Most Holy Lord.

It is impossible, from an earthly point of view, to worship and praise the Holy God as adequately as He deserves to be worshiped. It is hoped that one day there may be a moment when there will be participation with the Angelic Chorus as the song cascades in the courts of heaven ---

Holy, Holy, Holy! Lord God, Almighty!

Worthy is the Lamb who was slain- to receive power, and riches, and wisdom, and strength – Honor, and Glory, and Blessing!

Table of Contents

New Perspective for Life

New life in Jesus Christ is one that is filled with expectation and joy. Realizing what it means to be born again and the process of growth is exciting. In John 3, an intellectual and teacher asked Jesus about this very truth. "Nicodemus said to him, 'How can a man be born when he is old? Can he enter a second time into his mother's womb and be born?'" There are two actions one must take to enter into new life in Jesus Christ, that is, to be born again. Romans 10:9-10, 13 specify what these actions are: "if you confess with your mouth that Jesus is Lord and believe in your heart that God raised him from the dead, you will be saved. For with the heart one believes and is justified, and with the mouth one confesses and is saved...For everyone who calls on the name of the Lord will be saved."

Action 1: Confess with your mouth that Jesus is Lord.

Action 2: Believe in your heart that God raised Him from the dead.

Result: You will be saved – for everyone who calls on the name of the Lord will be saved. This is as clear and absolute as it can get: Confess...Believe... Call – you will be saved; you have become a Christian. It is vital to understand that being a "Christian" is more than observing and maintaining rituals and traditions. The purpose of Life in Christ is found in the summary of what one must under- stand and appreciate regarding new life in Christ.

Note the following passages - - - II Corinthians 5:14-21 (NIV)

For Christ's love compels us, because we are convinced that one died for all, and therefore all died. And he died for all, that those who live should no longer live for themselves but for him who died for them and was raised again. So from now on we regard no one from a worldly point of view. Though we once regarded Christ in this way, we do so no longer. Therefore, if anyone is in Christ, he is a new creation; the old has gone, the new has come! All this is from God, who reconciled us to himself through Christ and gave us the ministry of reconciliation: that God was reconciling the world to himself in Christ, not counting men's sins against them. And he has committed to us the message of reconciliation. We are therefore Christ's ambassadors, as though God were making his appeal through us. We implore you on Christ's behalf: Be reconciled to God. God made him who had no sin to be sin for us, so that in him we might become the righteousness of God.

Two of the key factors in these verses are:

Verse 15 - And he died for all, that those who live should no longer live for themselves but for him who died for them and was raised again. The thrust is: "no longer live for themselves but for Him." It is a new life with a new purpose under new ownership and management.

Verse 21 - God made him who had no sin to be sin for us, so that in him we might become the righteousness of God. The thrust is: "we might become the righteousness of God." It is a new lifestyle with new behaviors and with a different focus in all life situations.

But now a righteousness from God, apart from law, has been made known, to which the Law and the Prophets testify. This righteousness from God comes through faith in Jesus Christ to all who believe. There is no difference, for all have sinned and fall short of the glory of God, and are justified freely by his grace through the redemption that came by Christ Jesus. God presented him as a sacrifice of atonement... (Romans 3:21-24).

The Westminster Confession of Faith includes the following as it pertains to the reason for man's need for the righteousness of God in Christ.

I.   Our first parents, being seduced by the subtlety and temptation of Satan, sinned, in eating the forbidden fruit. This their sin, God was pleased, according to his wise and holy counsel, to permit, having purposed to order it to his own glory.

II.   By this sin they fell from their original righteousness and communion with God, and so became dead in sin, and wholly defiled in all the parts and faculties of soul and body.

III.   They being the root of all mankind, the guilt of this sin was imputed; and the same death in sin, and corrupted nature, conveyed to all their posterity descending from them by ordinary generation.

IV.   From this original corruption, whereby we are utterly indisposed, disabled, and made opposite to all good, and wholly inclined to all evil, do proceed all actual transgressions.

V.   This corruption of nature, during this life, doth remain in those that are regenerated; and although it be, through Christ, pardoned, and mortified; yet both itself, and all the motions thereof, are truly and properly sin.

VI.   Every sin, both original and actual, being a transgression of the righteous law of God, and contrary thereunto, doth, in its own nature, bring guilt upon the sinner, whereby he is bound over to the wrath of God, and curse of the law, and so made subject to death, with all miseries spiritual, temporal, and eternal. (Chapter VI, Of the Fall of Man, of Sin, and of the Punishment Thereof)

God intervenes to provide for and bring to fallen man a "…righteousness from God that comes through faith in Jesus Christ to all who believe." It isn't because we've earned it, and surely not because we deserve it. Romans 3:24 emphasizes that one is "…justified freely by his grace through the redemption that came by Christ Jesus…" Once that has occurred, we find that new life in Christ begins. It is a process where old things pass away and all things are becoming new. It is a process that impacts one's vocabulary, thoughts, actions, mind-sets, activity, belief system. It is a radical transformation where one who has been dead in trespasses and sins has become a recipient of God's favor – his love, mercy and grace – receiving redemption in Christ and forgiveness for all sin.

Romans 5:1-4 explains the transformation with these words: "Therefore, there is now no condemnation for those who are in Christ Jesus, because through Christ Jesus the law of the Spirit of life set me free from the law of sin and death. For what the law was powerless to do in that it was weakened by the sinful nature, God did by sending his own Son in the likeness of sinful man to be a sin offering. And so he condemned sin in sinful man, in order that the righteous requirements of the law might be fully met in us, who do not live according to the sinful nature but according to the Spirit."

The words "…in order that the righteous requirements of the law might be fully met in us…" is the reality of Jesus Christ being the sacrifice – the offering – for my sin. The fact that we have been forgiven – the recipients of God's love, mercy and grace – is because The Righteous One, Jesus Christ, took upon Himself my sin and my unrighteousness. In that act and completed work of Jesus Christ on the Cross, two defining things transpired: (a)

Propitiation – Christ removes the penalty of our sin, and (b) Expiation.- Christ removes the guilt of our sin.

Propitiation is the satisfaction/appeasement of Divine Justice. This was stated in Isaiah 53: 10-11 (ESV), "Yet it was the will of the LORD to crush him; he has put him to grief; when his soul makes an offering for guilt, he shall see his offspring; he shall prolong his days; the will of the LORD shall prosper in his hand. Out of the anguish of his soul he shall see and be satisfied; by his knowledge shall the righteous one, my servant, make many to be accounted righteous, and he shall bear their iniquities.

Expiation is the means by which atonement is made, the act of making atonement. It is the act of God to purify one of sin. This is what it means to be justified, namely, one is declared Not Guilty before a Holy God.

Some of what occurs in this act of justification, remission of sins has taken place.

John 1:29 – Sins are taken away.   "The next day he saw Jesus coming toward him, and said, "Be- hold, the Lamb of God, who takes away the sin of the world!" Acts 3:19 – sins are blotted out, removed from the record "Repent therefore, and turn again, that your sins may be blotted out…"
Acts 22:16 – Sins have been washed away. "And now why do you wait? Rise and be baptized and wash away your sins, calling on his name."
Romans 4:7 – Sins have been covered by the Blood of Christ. "Blessed are those whose lawless deeds are forgiven, and whose sins are covered."
Romans 4:8 – Sins are no longer counted (imputed) against us. "blessed is the man against whom the Lord will not count his sin."

Romans 6:17-18 – Sins no longer hold one in bondage – we have been set free. "But thanks be to God, that you who were once slaves of sin have become obedient from the heart to the standard of teaching to which you were committed, and, having been set free from sin, have become slaves of righteousness."

II Peter 1:9 – Sins have been cleansed (purged) from us. "For whoever lacks these qualities is so nearsighted that he is blind, having forgotten that he was cleansed from his former sins."

Hebrews 1:3 – "He is the radiance of the glory of God and the exact imprint of his nature, and he upholds the universe by the word of his power. After making purification for sins, he sat down at the right hand of the Majesty on high."

Hebrews 8:12 – Sins are remembered no more. "For I will be merciful toward their iniquities, and I will remember their sins no more." This is reiterated in Hebrews 10:17, and the covenant assertion: "Their sins and lawless acts I will remember no more."

Psalm 103:8-12 – "The LORD is merciful and gracious, slow to anger and abounding in steadfast love. He will not always chide, nor will he keep his anger forever. He does not deal with us according to our sins, nor repay us according to our iniquities. For as high as the heavens are above the earth, so great is his steadfast love toward those who fear him; as far as the east is from the west, so far does he remove our transgressions from us." The Message paraphrase of Verse 12 is – "as far as sunrise is from sunset, he has separated us from our sins."

The Message paraphrase of Hebrews 10:17 is encouraging and helpful: "He concludes, I'll forever wipe the slate clean of their sins. Once sins are taken care of for good, there's no longer any need to offer sacrifices for them. So, friends, we can now - without hesitation - walk right up to God, into the Holy Place. Jesus has cleared the way by the blood of his sacrifice, acting as our priest before God. The curtain into God's presence is his body. So let's do it - full of belief, confident that we're presentable inside and out. Let's keep a firm grip on the promises that keep us going. He always keeps his word." The phrase – "the curtain into God's Presence is His body" – reminds us that we now have full access into the Holy Place, into the presence of Almighty God.

As we gain that entrance and access, the words of a contemporary worship chorus come to mind - - -

In Your presence - There is comfort In Your presence - There is peace when we seek to know Your heart we will find such blessed assurance in Your holy presence Lord.

This is all part of our Practical Awareness of Living In The Presence of God. This should be the Prayer Commitment and Focus every day – reminding oneself that the right and best way for living one's life is in the Holy Presence of the Lord.

Personal Study Questions - - - In II Corinthians 5:15 - -

What does it mean for you to die unto self?

What does it entail for you to live unto Christ?

On what basis do you believe you have been born again?

What evidence is there to demonstrate you are a new creature in Christ?

A Chorus to learn and sing each day is:

> With eternity's values in view, Lord.
> May I do each day's work for Jesus.
> With eternity's values in view.

Sing as the prayer of your heart:

Have Thine own way, Lord!
Have Thine own way!
Thou art the Potter, I am the clay.
Mold me and make me after Thy will,
While I am waiting, yielded and still.

Growing and Walking

It is amazing to be able to observe a newborn baby and the rapid changes that occur. Because of both nutrition and nurture, the baby gains strength, health, awareness, recognition, and a personality. Before long, the baby will determine how to roll over, get on his/her knees, try to crawl, attempt to pull up, and finally stand – a bit wobbly – but the legs have never had to do that before. Parents become very excited when the baby takes a first step. The baby may plop down several times before being able to take several steps. Parents do all they can to help their baby Grow and Walk. They want their child to become strong and functional.

There is something very similar in the life of one who has been born again. There are two verses that will serve as a springboard or background for this Chapter.

To Grow: I Peter 2:2 (ESV)
"Like newborn infants, long for the pure spiritual milk, that by it you may grow up into salvation—"

From the New Living Translation: "You must crave pure spiritual milk so that you can grow into the fullness of your salvation. Cry out for this nourishment as a baby cries for milk…"

To Walk: Colossians 2:6-7 (ESV)
"as you received Christ Jesus the Lord, so walk in him, rooted and built up in him and established in the faith…"

It would be tragic to see or have a newborn that was indifferent to having any nourishment. That sometimes is the case, albeit rare, when a baby lacks the ability to suck. In the majority of births, when the baby is ready for nourishment, there is a frantic desire to be fed. When a baby is breast-fed, there will be the rooting and desire for the nourishing milk from the Mother. It will not be long before additions have to be made to just milk. Different types of other foods are introduced into the baby's diet – cereal, strained fruits and vegetables, different strained meats, and other juices. Why? To enable the baby to continue to grow and become stronger. It requires care and oversight in addition to nutrition and the nurturing.

When the baby begins to stand and take the first steps, a whole new dimension of safety occurs. Things that are harmful to the infant are put up or secured; items that might be dangerous are removed; cabinet doors have latches put on them – all to maintain a safe environment that will enable the growth and development of the infant.

The parallels are obvious in the New Birth process of growth and development. The one who receives Jesus Christ as Savior and Lord needs to learn what that entails for one's life. There will need to be follow-up discipleship – the care and nurturing on a spiritual level. It begins with a hunger for the Word of God – the pure spiritual milk, that by it one may grow up – learning the ramifications and requirements of salvation. There needs to be evidence of progress in growth as one is nourished by and from the Word of God. It will keep in mind, that even though the process begins with the pure milk of the word, it doesn't and cannot be just that diet.

There is a section in Hebrews that contains this input for the ongoing growth and development of the believer.

Hebrews 5:12-14 (ESV)
"For though by this time you ought to be teachers, you need someone to teach you again the basic principles of the oracles of God. You need milk, not solid food, for everyone who lives on

milk is unskilled in the word of righteousness, since he is a child. But solid food is for the mature, for those who have their powers of discernment trained by constant practice to distinguish good from evil."

There is the time and place to move on to the solid food that will bring about spiritual maturity. It is moving from milk as the sole and exclusive source of nourishment to the diet of that which is more substantial – the meat of the Word. This is echoed in the following chapter - -

Hebrews 6:1-2 (ESV)
"…let us leave the elementary doctrine of Christ and go on to maturity, not laying again a foundation of repentance from dead works and of faith toward God, and of instruction about washings, the laying on of hands, the resurrection of the dead, and eternal judgment."

The writer of Hebrews is teaching about personal growth and development in spiritual matters. One has to learn the basics – the foundational truths, but there has to be a focus on a personal relationship with Jesus Christ. Note the following - - -

Ephesians 5:1-2
"…be imitators of God, as beloved children. And walk in love, as Christ loved us and gave himself up for us, a fragrant offering and sacrifice to God."

Ephesians 5:8-10
"Walk as children of light (for the fruit of light is found in all that is good and right and true), and try to discern what is pleasing to the Lord."

Ephesians 5:15-18
"Look carefully then how you walk, not as unwise but as wise, making the best use of the time, because the days are evil. Therefore do not be foolish, but understand what the will of the Lord is. And...be filled with the Spirit"

What exactly is meant by understanding what the will of the Lord is, and to be filled with the Spirit? The following verses give us some insight - - -

Galatians 5:16-25 (ESV – Selected)
"...walk by the Spirit, and you will not gratify the desires of the flesh. For the desires of the flesh are against the Spirit, and the desires of the Spirit are against the flesh, for these are opposed to each other, to keep you from doing the things you want to do. But if you are led by the Spirit, you are not under the law. Now the works of the flesh are evident: sexual immorality, impurity, sensuality, idolatry, sorcery, enmity, strife, jealousy, fits of anger, rivalries, dissensions, divisions, envy, drunkenness, orgies, and things like these. I warn you, as I warned you before, that those who do such things will not inherit the kingdom of God. But the fruit of the Spirit is love, joy, peace, patience, kindness, goodness, faithfulness, gentleness, self-control; against such things there is no law. And those who belong to Christ Jesus have crucified the flesh with its passions and desires. If we live by the Spirit, let us also walk by the Spirit."

Why does one need growth and development in spiritual areas of and for life – in all areas of life? Primarily, because there is a spiritual conflict, a war, being waged for the souls of people. It is between the things of the flesh versus the things of the Spirit. It is the carnal versus the Spiritual. It is between that which will tear down versus that which will build up. The above text states it as: "For the desires of the flesh are against the Spirit, and the desires of the Spirit are against the flesh, for these are opposed to each other, to keep you from doing the things you want to do." How can one survive spiritually through such a conflict?

The primary answers are: (1) to Walk by the Spirit, (2) to be Led by the Spirit, and (3) to be filled with the Fruit of the Spirit.

To Walk by the Spirit – means to walk by His enablement and under His control.

To be Led by the Spirit – means that we are enabled to conquer sin in the present tense.

To Be filled with the Fruit of the Spirit – means we give evidence of the ongoing spiritual growth as that fruit is displayed in, by and through the child of God – the nine spiritual attributes of: love, joy, peace, patience, kindness, goodness, faithfulness, gentleness, self-control.

The summary in Galatians 5 is: "If we live by the Spirit, let us also walk by the Spirit." The One Who Leads Us and Fill Us must be The One Who Guides Us and enables us to walk by His enablement. This is further amplified when Paul wrote to the Church at Rome.

Romans 8:12-17 (ESV)
"So then, brothers, we are debtors, not to the flesh, to live according to the flesh. For if you live according to the flesh you will die, but if by the Spirit you put to death the deeds of the body, you will live. For all who are led by the Spirit of God are sons of God. For you did not receive the spirit of slavery to fall back into fear, but you have received the Spirit of adoption as sons, by whom we cry, Abba! Father! The Spirit himself bears witness with our spirit that we are children of God, and if children, then heirs--heirs of God and fellow heirs with Christ, provided we suffer with him in order that we may also be glorified with him."

As one grows in the Lord and walks by the enablement of The Spirit, there is this basic statement regarding salvation and what it means: "...For all who are led by the Spirit of God are sons of God. For you did not receive the spirit of slavery to fall back into fear, but you have received the Spirit of adoption as sons, by whom we cry, Abba! Father! The Spirit himself bears witness with our spirit that we are children of God, and if children, then...heirs of God and fellow heirs with Christ..."

The measure of where one is in terms of relationship to Jesus Christ, as well as in the Growth and Development that is taking place, is reiterated here - - -

(1)   All who are led by the Spirit of God are sons of God. No one can claim to be a child of God unless and until measurable evidence can demonstrate one is being led by the Spirit of God.

(2)   The Spirit bears witness with our spirit that we are children of God. It is the inner assurance that new life has begun and there is ongoing maturity taking place. One is becoming strong in the Lord and in the strength of His might.

In this process of Spirit-Leading and Spirit-Witnessing, there are areas in which one must be very careful and guarded. Part of the instruction is that one needs to be sensitive to the things of the Spirit. No one has the luxury of ignoring the Spirit and embracing only that which one decides to pick and choose for one's life. For instance, consider these words - - -

The Danger Of Grieving and Quenching The Spirit

Grieving - Ephesians 4:30-32 (ESV)

"And do not grieve the Holy Spirit of God, by whom you were sealed for the day of redemption. Let all bitterness and wrath and anger and clamor and slander be put away from you, along with all malice. Be kind to one another, tenderhearted, forgiving one another, as God in Christ forgave you."

Aside from the fact that we have been sealed by Him for the day of redemption, how can and does one grieve the Spirit? The answer given is: "Let all bitterness, wrath, anger, clamor and slander be put away from you, along with all malice."

Bitterness embraces all of the other negative behaviors that will Grieve the Holy Spirit because it is a devastating mental attitude that triggers a wide range of other sins, such as, Hatred, Cruelty, Antagonism, Self-pity, Vindictiveness and desires for revenge, Prideful ambition (arrogance). Bitterness disrupts one's personal fellowship with the Lord; delays and withholds blessings that could've been bestowed upon one; interrupts personal development and growth; and separates one from having fellowship with those of like precious faith.

Hebrews 12:15 warns: "See to it that no one fails to obtain the grace of God; that no root of bitterness springs up and causes trouble, and by it many become defiled..."

Quenching - I Thessalonians 5:19-22
"Do not quench the Spirit. Do not despise prophecies, but test everything; hold fast what is good. Abstain from every form of evil.."

Charles Finney, a Presbyterian Revivalist of the 19th Century, shares his view on how one may Quench the Holy Spirit of God:

1.   Men often quench the Spirit by directly resisting the truth he presents to their minds.

2.   The Spirit is often quenched by endeavoring to support error.
3.   By uncharitable judgments.
4.   The Spirit. is grieved by harsh and vituperative language.
5.   The Spirit of God is quenched by a bad temper.
6.   Often the Spirit is quenched by diverting the attention from the truth.
7.   We often quench the Spirit by indulging intemperate excitement on any subject.
8.   The Spirit is quenched by indulging prejudice.
9.   The Spirit is often quenched by violating conscience.
10.   Persons often quench the Spirit by indulging their appetites and passions.
11.   The Spirit is often quenched by indulging in dishonesty.
12.   Often men quench the Spirit by casting off fear and restraining prayer.
13.   The Spirit is quenched by idle conversation.
14.   Men quench the Holy Ghost by a spirit of levity and trifling.
15.   It is to be feared that many have quenched the Spirit by resisting the doctrine and duty of sanctification.

Finney goes on to address the consequences of quenching the Holy Spirit:

1.   Great darkness of mind. Abandoned of God, the mind sees truth so dimly that it makes no useful impression.
2.   There usually results great coldness and stupidity in regard to religion generally. It leaves to the mind no such interest in spiritual things as men take in worldly things.
3.   The mind falls very naturally into diverse errors in religion. The heart wanders from God, loses its hold on the truth, and perhaps the man insists that he now takes a much more liberal and enlightened view of the subject than before.

4. Quenching the Spirit often results in infidelity
5. Another result is great hardness of heart.
6. Another result is deep delusion in regard to their spiritual state.
7. Persons in this state often justify themselves in most manifest wrong, because they put darkness for light and light for darkness.

Charles Finney touched upon areas that should cause concern in terms of whether or not one is growing cold to the things of God and are – in effect or fact - Quenching the Spirit of God. Quench means to put out or extinguish; to subdue, destroy, overcome, quell.

The verses in Ephesians 4 and I Thessalonians 5 are instructing us to avoid the behaviors that would Grieve the Holy Spirit, and to remove oneself from those people and situations that would expose one to the activities that will Quench the Holy Spirit.

Just these final thoughts - - -

Colossians 1:9-10
"…we have not ceased to pray for you, asking that you may be filled with the knowledge of his will in all spiritual wisdom and understanding, so as to walk in a manner worthy of the Lord, fully pleasing to him, bearing fruit in every good work and increasing in the knowledge of God.

I John 1:5-7
"This is the message we have heard from him and proclaim to you, that God is light, and in him is no darkness at all. If we say we have fellowship with him while we walk in darkness, we lie and do not practice the truth. But if we walk in the light, as he is in the light, we have fellowship with one another, and the blood of Jesus his Son cleanses us from all sin.

May God grant that this represents the reality and commitment of your life both now and forevermore.

Personal Study Questions - - -

When you read your Bible, do you have a Bible Dictionary and Concordance handy?

Have you been involved in anything that would have grieved the Holy Spirit? What did you do about it?

Have you ever been guilty of quenching the Holy Spirit? How and what did you do about it?

If someone else made an a spiritual assessment of your life, what do you think they would say about you? Why?

Are you filled with the knowledge of God's will – or – are still rooting for milk instead of meat?

Have you grown spiritually and significantly in the past twelve months? How – or Why Not?

Training and Learning

There is a basic text in the process of Training and Learning – Proverbs 22:6, "Train up a child in the way he should go; even when he is old he will not depart from it." Someone has wisely said, "The training up of a child is an adult decision…" On the Dr. Henry Brandt webpage is this introductory statement: "Life is hard. It can be even harder without teaching and guidance to deal biblically with life's problems. God often uses trials to strengthen the faith of His children and teach them His ways. But believers need God's perspective on how to cure their problems, so they can become the fruitful disciples that God desires."

When we fully understand and appreciate how wonderfully we have been made by God, we realize that the interaction of body, soul and spirit is complex. When the wise parent endeavors to train up the child in terms of direction and values for life, the complexity becomes obvious. As beautiful and lovely and cuddly a baby may be, the fact is this infant has been born with a mind, emotions and a will. Early on, the infant will manifest things that he/she is thinking, feeling and wanting. The wise and Biblical parent will respond accordingly. However, if one is not careful and wise, that innocent and adorable baby will begin to train the parents for it's wants and desires. Loving a child does not mean the parents should yield to the child's demands via sounds, and later on – words.

The same process for the training of a child is magnified for the child of God and learning the lessons of what it means to be "trained in righteousness." The positive thrust in the lives of God's children is to the end that they learn how to become obedient to the will of God. It is obvious that this is an ongoing learning process as one "more and more dies unto sin, and lives unto righteousness." (See: Westminster Shorter Catechism 35). The negative aspect is an application from the prophecy of Jeremiah about idolatry in the land. It becomes sound counsel for the people of God today and all of the societal pressures within our culture. We are not to be numbered among the godless but among only the godly. Because we live in this world, we are not to be of this world. We are to represent and live as light shining in darkness. Note the words of the Prophet:

Jeremiah 10:1-3 (Selected) - "Hear the word that the Lord speaks to you...Thus says the Lord: Learn not the way of the nations, nor be dismayed at the signs of the heavens because the nations are dismayed at them, for the customs of the peoples are vanity..."

The Message Paraphrase - "Listen to the Message that God is sending your way...Listen most carefully: Don't take the godless nations as your models. Don't be impressed by their glamour and glitz, no matter how much they're impressed. The religion of these peoples is nothing but smoke..."

The idea of Discipline does not just refer to a form of corporal punishment administered randomly by the parent. The Bible allows there is a time and place for it. The idea of "spare the rod and spoil the child" is based upon Biblical precepts and concepts. Just a couple of examples are – Proverbs 13:24 -

"Whoever spares the rod hates his son, but he who loves him is diligent to discipline him."

In Proverbs 23:12-15 – "Apply your heart to instruction and your ear to words of knowledge. Do not withhold discipline from a child; if you strike him with a rod, he will not die. If you strike him with the rod, you will save his soul from hell. My son, if your heart is wise, my heart too will be glad.

The New Living Translation

"Commit yourself to instruction; attune your ears to hear words of knowledge. Don't fail to correct your children. They won't die if you spank them. Physical discipline may well save them from death. My child, how I will rejoice if you become wise."

The Message Paraphrase

"Give yourselves to disciplined instruction; open your ears to tested knowledge. Don't be afraid to correct your young ones; a spanking won't kill them. A good spanking, in fact, might save them from something worse than death. Dear child, if you become wise, I'll be one happy parent."

Parents must be very guarded in how and why spanking occurs and is administered. A special word of instruction is given to parents and children, and a word of caution is given to the Father in Ephesians 6:1-4, "Children, obey your parents in the Lord, for this is right. Honor your father and mother (this is the first commandment with a promise), that it may go well with you and that you may live long in the land. Fathers, do not provoke your children to anger, but bring them up in the discipline and instruction of the Lord."

The Message Paraphrase states: "Children, do what your parents tell you. This is only right. Honor your father and mother is the first commandment that has a promise attached to it, namely, so you will live well and have a long life. Fathers, don't exasperate your children by coming down hard on them. Take them by the hand and lead them in the way of the Master." This last phrase is tremendous as we are involved in the nurturing process - "Take them by the hand, and lead them to the Master."

We don't want to ignore this aspect of discipline, namely spanking, nor should we ignore the bigger picture of discipline. Discipline also includes the process by which one becomes a learner of a lifestyle and value system. A teacher knows that precepts and concepts are more caught than taught and will accomplish the greatest result by training in that way. It is how the Lord Jesus Christ trained His disciples. Note what He said in – Luke 6:39-40 - "He also told them a parable: Can a blind man lead a blind man? Will they not both fall into a pit? A disciple is not above his teacher, but everyone when he is fully trained will be like his teacher."

The key is that the "fully trained" disciple will be like his Lord, Master and Teacher. The Teacher models the reality of what a disciple is to know, think and do. The Teacher models it and the Disciple embraces and follows it.

A meaningful picture is drawn of The Potter and the Clay in – Jeremiah 18:1-6 - "The word that came to Jeremiah from the Lord: Arise, and go down to the potter's house, and there I will let you hear my words. So I went down to the potter's house, and there he was working at his wheel. And the vessel he was making of clay was spoiled in the potter's hand, and he reworked it into another vessel, as it seemed good to the potter to do. Then the word of the Lord came to me: O house of Israel, can I not do with you as this potter has done? declares the Lord. Behold, like the clay in the potter's hand, so are you in my hand," This idea of The Potter and the Clay is also referred to in – Isaiah 64:4-8 - "From of old no one has heard or perceived by the ear, no eye has seen a God besides you, who acts for those who wait for him. You meet him who joyfully works righteousness, those who remember you in your ways. Behold, you were angry, and we sinned; in our sins we have been a long time, and shall we be saved? We have all become like one who is unclean, and all our righteous deeds are like a polluted garment. We all fade like a leaf, and our iniquities, like the wind, take us away. There is no one who calls upon your name, who rouses himself to take hold of you; for you have hidden your face from us, and have made us melt in the hand of our iniquities. But now, O Lord, you are our Father; we are the clay, and you are our potter; we are all the work of your hand."

The picture Isaiah draws is – The Father as The Potter, shaping the clay – His children, so they become the work of His hand and showing forth His righteousness. It occurs as one is in the presence of the Father and Potter and knowing His touch and shaping our lives into useful and useable vessels. Many years ago, someone captured the meaning of this and penned the words of a Commitment Chorus - -

> Only to be what He wants me to be,
> Every moment of every day,
> Yielded completely to Jesus alone
> Every step of this pilgrim way.
> Just to be clay in the Potter's hands,
> Ready to do what His will demands
> Only to be what He wants me to be,
> Every moment of every day,

There is an important quality for the life of the one seeking to know what it means to live in the presence of God. It does not happen automatically or immediately, nor does it happen through osmosis. It will only occur by means of commitment, training and discipline. An important background text is - Hebrews 12:5-11 (ESV) - "…have you forgotten the exhortation that addresses you as sons? "My son, do not regard lightly the discipline of the Lord, nor be weary when reproved by him. For the Lord disciplines the one he loves, and chastises every son whom he receives. It is for discipline that you have to endure. God is treating you as sons. For what son is there whom his father does not discipline? If you are left without discipline, in which all have participated, then you are illegitimate children and not sons. Besides this, we have had earthly fathers who disciplined us and we respected them. Shall we not much more be subject to the Father of spirits and live? For they disciplined us for a short time as it seemed best to them, but he disciplines us for our good, that we may share his holiness. For the moment all discipline seems painful rather than pleasant, but later it yields the peaceful fruit of righteousness to those who have been trained by it."

Another of these important texts is – II Timothy 3:14-17 -

"But as for you, continue in what you have learned and have firmly believed, knowing from whom you learned it and how from childhood you have been acquainted with the sacred writings, which are able to make you wise for salvation through faith in Christ Jesus. All Scripture is breathed out by God and profitable for teaching, for reproof, for correction, and for training in righteousness, that the man of God may be competent, equipped for every good work."

Here again, importance is stated in terms of "training in righteousness" so that the child of God will be competent and equipped. There should never be resentment that this training is taking place, but rather rejoicing that one is being loved in such a way that his/her life is being shaped to be like the Teacher and Master – the Lord Jesus Christ. The purposes of God in this training is always for one's good. The expected response of the child of God is Love and Thanksgiving.

There was an instruction given to Timothy – I Timothy 4:4-7,

"For everything created by God is good, and nothing is to be rejected if it is received with thanksgiving, for it is made holy by the word of God and prayer. If you put these things before the brothers, you will be a good servant of Christ Jesus, being trained in the words of the faith and of the good doctrine that you have followed. Have nothing to do with irreverent, silly myths. Rather train yourself for godliness…"

There is the instruction, counsel and discipline – the ongoing "training in righteousness" and "train yourself to be godly."

As the Lord was delivering His people from Egypt, He gave His people a command with an explanation –

Deuteronomy 11:1-9 (Selected)

"You shall therefore love the Lord your God and keep his charge, his statutes, his rules, and his commandments always. And…consider the discipline of the Lord your God, his greatness, his mighty hand and his outstretched arm, his signs and his deeds…and what he did to the army of Egypt, to their horses and to their chariots…and what he did to you in the wilderness, until you came to this place…For your eyes have seen all the great work of the Lord that he did. You shall therefore keep the whole commandment that I command you today, that you may be strong, and go in and take possession of the land that you are going over to possess, and that you may live long in the land that the Lord swore to your fathers to give to them and to their offspring, a land flowing with milk and honey…"

The Lord is reminding them of all He has done for them in their training, discipline, adapting and applying His examples and His Commandments. He is reminding them of the principle that He is the Potter and they are the clay. He is the one who is molding and shaping them into what He wants them to be and where He wants them to go. To be molded into His likeness should be the goal and commitment of every child of God. How one responds to this training and learning process determines the kind of person or vessel we will become. Can you imagine a lump of clay with a resistant mindset or will – refusing to be shaped and molded by the Potter? Can you visualize a lump of clay that is unyielding to the Master's touch and unwilling to be shaped by the Potter – just resistant, rigid, shapeless, useless? As we pursue what it means to practice the presence of God and to live daily in the presence of God, we will need to read and heed God's instruction and direction for us. We cannot assert that we have arrived at that place and station in life. However, it will be observable by others – whether or not we think it, feel it, or not – just as Moses glowed with the glory of from having been in God's presence on the mountain – there will be a radiance glowing from the child of God who is devoted to being with and spending quality time in the presence of our Lord and Savior, Jesus Christ.

Personal Study Questions - - -

How much quality time do you spend in the presence of the Lord each day?

Do others hear you merely speaking about Jesus, or do they see Jesus reflected by you in your words, deeds and actions?

Do you consider yourself to be clay that the Potter can mold and make into what He wants it to be, or do you resist the touch of the Potter's hand because you are content in your comfort zone and what you deem yourself to be?

Are you teachable or do you believe you already know all that anyone needs to know?

Conformed and Conforming

To be a new creation in Christ Jesus entails conversion, growth, transformation – and – a reconstruction of the inner being - that occurs as old things are passing away and all things are becoming new. There is a new beginning and a continuing process as the necessary changes are effected and implemented. Romans 8:28-30 gives a broad idea of what has and what will occur.

"And we know that for those who love God all things work together for good, for those who are called according to his purpose. For those whom he foreknew he also predestined to be conformed to the image of his Son, in order that he might be the firstborn among many brothers. And those whom he predestined he also called, and those whom he called he also justified, and those whom he justified he also glorified."

The key phrase being singled out here is "conformed to the image of His Son." What does that mean? What does it entail? How can it be achieved? To answer these questions, the following background will be of assistance.

Ephesians 4:20-24

"But that is not the way you learned Christ! assuming that you have heard about him and were taught in him, as the truth is in Jesus, to put off your old self, which belongs to your former manner of life and is corrupt through deceitful desires, and to be renewed in the spirit of your minds, and to put on the new self, created after the likeness of God in true righteousness and holiness."

To be conformed to the image of His Son means to be "created after the likeness of God in true righteousness and holiness." The thrust is (a) true righteousness and (b) true holiness. Jesus made a startling statement during His Sermon on the Mount. In Matthew 5:20 – Jesus said, "For I tell you, unless your righteousness exceeds that of the scribes and Pharisees, you will never enter the kingdom of heaven." The context both before and after this statement by Jesus focuses on The Law and The Prophets. Matthew 5:19, Jesus stated – "Therefore whoever relaxes one of the least of these commandments and teaches others to do the same will be called least in the kingdom of heaven, but whoever does them and teaches them will be called great in the kingdom of heaven." Everything that follows in Matthew 5 is an amplification and application of The Moral Law of God emphasizing - - - Anger as a correlation to Murder; And Lust as a correlation to Adultery. He then speaks about Divorce and how it can lead to Adultery; Oaths and how they can be borderline with Evil; Retaliation and the discipline to resist it; and a Choice and Commitment to Love one's neighbor.

This portion of the Sermon on the Mount closes with these words in Matthew 5:48, "You therefore must be perfect, as your heavenly Father is perfect."

There are places in Scripture where the emphasis is upon The Law of God and why it should be incorporated into a persons life. Consider these passages of Scripture in that regard - - -

Joshua 1:6-9 - the Lord gives Joshua instruction, guidance and reassurance to Joshua as he assumes Leadership following the death of Moses.

"Be strong and courageous, for you shall cause this people to inherit the land that I swore to their fathers to give them. Only be strong and very courageous, being careful to do according to all the law that Moses my servant commanded you. Do not turn from it to the right hand or to the left, that you may have good success wherever you go. This Book of the Law shall not depart from your mouth, but you shall meditate on it day and night, so that you may be careful to do according to all that is written in it. For then you will make your way prosperous, and then you will have good success. Have I not commanded you? Be strong and courageous. Do not be frightened, and do not be dismayed, for the LORD your God is with you wherever you go." Three of the Key Aspects are - - -

(1)   Be strong and courageous – it is a big responsibility and venture.
(2)   Be Careful to do according to all the Law that Moses my servant commanded you – no deviation or altering of the prescribed standard of God.
(3)   Meditate on the Law constantly – it will make your way prosperous, and then you will have good success.

Psalm 1:1-3 where we are given a summary necessary for one's life, as well as an introduction to and summary of the Book of Psalms. Note what is tantamount to the growth and success for the godly person - - -

"Blessed is the man who walks not in the counsel of the wicked, nor stands in the way of sinners, nor sits in the seat of scoffers; but his delight is in the law of the Lord, and on his law he meditates day and night. He is like a tree planted by streams of water that yields its fruit in its season, and its leaf does not wither. In all that he does, he prospers.

(1)   The Careful Walk – avoiding the wicked, the sinner, and the scoffer.
(2)   The Careful Choice – delighting in the Law of the Lord.

(3)   The Careful Discipline – meditating in God's Law day and night.

(4)   The Careful Nourishment – planted by the streams of water so one will flourish and be fruitful.

(5)   The Reality and Result – in all that he does he prospers.

Once again, it is promised and assured success for the one living his/her life in accord with God's precepts and purpose.

All of this is foundational if one is ever going to experience true righteousness and holiness.

We have three powerful concepts and requirements for the one desiring to follow Jesus Christ, namely, True Righteousness, True Holiness, Being Perfect.

Some glimpses into what the Scriptures speak of and teach about Righteousness - - -

II Timothy 3:16-17, "All Scripture is breathed out by God and profitable for teaching, for reproof, for correction, and for training in righteousness, that the man of God may be competent, equipped for every good work." The thrust: The Scriptures are profitable for "training in righteousness."

To determine what true righteousness is, we need to know what it means to be righteous. Strong's Concordance lists these ideas and definitions:

(1)   to be righteous is observing divine laws - in a wide sense, it means to be upright, righteous, virtuous, keeping the commands of God

(2)   to be righteous is to be innocent, faultless, guiltless

(3)   to be righteous is to be used of him whose way of thinking, feeling, and acting is wholly conformed to the will of

God, and who therefore needs no rectification in the heart or life, namely, only Christ truly

(4)   to be righteous means to be approved of or acceptable of God. In a narrower sense, rendering to each his due and that in a judicial sense, passing just judgment on others, whether expressed in words or shown by the manner of dealing with them.

There are numerous examples of those who were deemed to be righteous. A few of them who were so characterized and noted are the following (some are listed in Hebrews 11):

Abel - Hebrews 11:4
"By faith Abel offered to God a more acceptable sacrifice than Cain, through which he was commended as righteous, God commending him by accepting his gifts. And through his faith, though he died, he still speaks." He was "commended as righteous" because he offered acceptable gifts to God, namely, the blood sacrifice.

Noah - Hebrews 11:7
"By faith Noah, being warned by God concerning events as yet unseen, in reverent fear constructed an ark for the saving of his household. By this he condemned the world and became an heir of the righteousness that comes by faith."

Genesis 6:9 affirms, "Noah was a righteous man, blameless in his generation. Noah walked with God."

Genesis 7:1, "Then the LORD said to Noah, Go into the ark, you and all your household, for I have seen that you are righteous before me in this generation."

"True righteousness is finding favor in God's eyes. Noah was in the world but not of it. He was not like the generation he lived in.

Because of his righteousness he and his family were saved while the rest of the world was destroyed in the flood.

Abraham - Hebrews 11:8-10
"By faith Abraham obeyed when he was called to go out to a place that he was to receive as an inheritance. And he went out, not knowing where he was going. By faith he went to live in the land of promise, as in a foreign land, living in tents with Isaac and Jacob, heirs with him of the same promise. For he was looking forward to the city that has foundations, whose designer and builder is God."

We gain an insight into "true righteousness" in Abraham's life in .In Genesis 18:22-33. Abraham intercedes for Sodom. He does so because his nephew Lot is living there with his family. In this passage, we read about Abraham's request of God to spare the city if some righteous people could be found there.

"Abraham still stood before the Lord. Then Abraham drew near and said, Will you indeed sweep away the righteous with the wicked? Suppose there are fifty righteous within the city. Will you then sweep away the place and not spare it for the fifty righteous who are in it? Far be it from you to do such a thing, to put the righteous to death with the wicked, so that the righteous fare as the wicked! Far be that from you! Shall not the Judge of all the earth do what is just? And the Lord said, If I find at Sodom fifty righteous in the city, I will spare the whole place for their sake.

"Abraham answered and said, Behold, I have undertaken to speak to the Lord, I who am but dust and ashes. Suppose five of the fifty righteous are lacking. Will you destroy the whole city for lack of five? And he said, I will not destroy it if I find forty-five there."

"Again he spoke to him and said, Suppose forty are found there. He answered, For the sake of forty I will not do it.

"Then he said, Oh let not the Lord be angry, and I will speak. Suppose thirty are found there. He answered, I will not do it, if I find thirty there.

He said, Behold, I have undertaken to speak to the Lord. Suppose twenty are found there. He answered, For the sake of twenty I will not destroy it.

Then he said, Oh let not the Lord be angry, and I will speak again but this once. Suppose ten are found there. He answered, For the sake of ten I will not destroy it.

"And the Lord went his way, when he had finished speaking to Abraham, and Abraham returned to his place."

The heart of Abraham wanted to spare the righteous if they could be found. The Lord had to convince Abraham that there were none to be found. As Romans 3:10-12 declares, "..."None is righteous, no, not one; no one understands; no one seeks for God. All have turned aside; together they have become worthless; no one does good, not even one."

What is it when one has True Righteousness?

In Luke 1:5-6 – We read that "...there was a priest named Zechariah, of the division of Abijah. And he had a wife from the daughters of Aaron, and her name was Elizabeth. And they were both righteous before God, walking blamelessly in all the commandments and statutes of the Lord."

What Is True Righteousness?

It is having strong faith in God and being totally obedient to Him.

What is the Bible's Description of one who possesses True Righteousness?

1 Peter 3:10-12 – A Changed Behavior
"Whoever desires to love life and see good days, let him keep his tongue from evil and his lips from speaking deceit; let him turn away from evil and do good; let him seek peace and pursue it. For the eyes of the Lord are on the righteous, and his ears are open to their prayer. But the face of the Lord is against those who do evil."

Description:

* Keeps his tongue from evil and his lips from speaking deceit.
* Turns away from evil and does good.
* Seeks peace and pursues it.

I John 3:6-10 – The Result of one who is Abiding In Christ

"No one who abides in him keeps on sinning; no one who keeps on sinning has either seen him or known him. Little children, let no one deceive you. Whoever practices righteousness is righteous, as he is righteous. Whoever makes a practice of sinning is of the devil, for the devil has been sinning from the beginning. The reason the Son of God appeared was to destroy the works of the devil. No one born of God makes a practice of sinning, for God's seed abides in him, and he cannot keep on sinning because he has been born of God. By this it is evident who are the children of God, and who are the children of the devil: whoever does not practice righteousness is not of God, nor is the one who does not love his brother."

Key: "Whoever practices righteousness is righteous, as he is righteous…. whoever does not practice righteousness is not of God…"

This is as clear and precise as possible. There is no in-between. There can be no gray area. There can be no sometimes righteous and sometimes not righteous. Someone defined righteousness as a totality in one's life impacting the areas of one's integrity, virtue, purity of life, rightness, correctness of thinking, feeling, and acting. We must always remember the instruction of Jesus Christ in The Sermon on the Mount – Matthew 5:6, "Blessed are those who hunger and thirst for righteousness, for they shall be satisfied – they shall be filled."

There are many areas in Scripture that direct one toward living righteously and how it affects one's worship and receiving the care and blessing of God.

Example: Psalm 34:15
"The eyes of the LORD are on the righteous and his ears are attentive to their cry…"

Example: Psalm 4:5 (NKJV)
"Offer the sacrifices of righteousness, And put your trust in the Lord."

Example: Hebrews 12:11
"Now no chastening seems to be joyful for the present, but painful; nevertheless, afterward it yields the peaceable fruit of righteousness to those who have been trained by it."

Example: Ephesians 5:8-10
"For you were once darkness, but now you are light in the Lord. Walk as children of light (for the fruit of the Spirit is in all

goodness, righteousness, and truth), finding out what is acceptable to the Lord."

Two other passages that address one's being conformed to the image of Jesus Christ are:

Colossians 3:9-10 (NKJV)
"Do not lie to one another, since you have put off the old man with his deeds, and have put on the new man who is renewed in knowledge according to the image of Him who created him..."

Romans 12:1-3 (NKJV)
"I beseech you therefore, brethren, by the mercies of God, that you present your bodies a living sacrifice, holy, acceptable to God, which is your reasonable service. And do not be conformed to this world, but be transformed by the renewing of your mind, that you may prove what is that good and acceptable and perfect will of God. For I say, through the grace given to me, to everyone who is among you, not to think of himself more highly than he ought to think, but to think soberly, as God has dealt to each one a measure of faith.."

In all of these passages, righteousness is to be the reality in our lives. It is not to be merely spoken about, or acted out similar to the Pharisees, but that which flows fully and constantly because of being related and one in Jesus Christ – The Righteous One.

The consideration of "being holy" and "being perfect" will be discussed in following chapters.

Personal Study Questions - - -

What is your definition of righteousness?

Is righteousness something that you can more easily exhibit in a church setting, or is it a constant in all your associations – home, work, school, social events?

If someone asked you how they could become righteous, what would your answer and instruction be?

Do you have a personal sense that "the eyes of the Lord are on the righteous and he is attentive to your prayers?

Prepared and Ready

The Lord Jesus Christ spoke clearly about the reality of His coming again. He indicated no specific time – just the fact that at a precise moment He would return. He makes a statement contained in the adage: "A word to the wise is sufficient." Note His words in Matthew 24:44, "Therefore you also must be ready, for the Son of Man is coming at an hour you do not expect." An unexpected moment – an unexpected hour – He is coming.

In terms of being prepared, He teaches them in Matthew 25:1-13, The Parable of the Virgins. The text records - - - "Then the kingdom of heaven will be like ten virgins who took their lamps and went to meet the bridegroom. Five of them were foolish, and five were wise. For when the foolish took their lamps, they took no oil with them, but the wise took flasks of oil with their lamps. As the bridegroom was delayed, they all became drowsy and slept. But at midnight there was a cry, Here is the bridegroom! Come out to meet him. Then all those virgins rose and trimmed their lamps. And the foolish said to the wise, Give us some of your oil, for our lamps are going out. But the wise answered, saying, Since there will not be enough for us and for you, go rather to the dealers and buy for yourselves. And while they were going to buy, the bridegroom came, and those who were ready went in with him to the marriage feast, and the door was shut. Afterward the other virgins came also, saying, Lord, lord, open to us. But he answered, Truly, I say to you, I do not know you. Watch therefore, for you know neither the day nor the hour." Once again the sense of urgency is given, namely, Be Watchful inasmuch as you don't know the day or hour when the Bridegroom will return.

The other part of preparedness and readiness is to know where the Lord Jesus Christ is going to take you. In John 14:1-3, Jesus told His followers: "Let not your hearts be troubled. Believe in God; believe also in me. In my Father's house are many rooms. If it were not so, would I have told you that I go to prepare a place for you? And if I go and prepare a place for you, I will come again and will take you to myself, that where I am you may be also." The place that is prepared for us – what goes on there? What will be occurring?

We get a glimpse of one activity in Heaven from Isaiah 6:1-7, Isaiah shares a vision he had of the Lord and Heaven: "I saw the Lord sitting upon a throne, high and lifted up; and the train of his robe filled the temple. Above him stood the seraphim. Each had six wings: with two he covered his face, and with two he covered his feet, and with two he flew. And one called to another and said: Holy, holy, holy is the Lord of hosts; the whole earth is full of his glory! And the foundations of the thresholds shook at the voice of him who called, and the house was filled with smoke. And I said: Woe is me! For I am lost; for I am a man of unclean lips, and I dwell in the midst of a people of unclean lips; for my eyes have seen the King, the Lord of hosts! Then one of the seraphim flew to me, having in his hand a burning coal that he had taken with tongs from the altar. And he touched my mouth and said: Behold, this has touched your lips; your guilt is taken away, and your sin atoned for."

In this vision, we learn that it is a place of continuous Worship. The heavens reverberate with the sound of the Seraphim as they sang out to each other – "Holy, holy, holy is the Lord of hosts; the whole earth is full of his glory!" It is a place of Holiness – a place of purity. When the seraphim brought a coal from the altar, he touched it upon his lips and exclaimed: "Behold, this has touched your lips; your guilt is taken away, and your sin atoned for." It is a place where Guilt has been removed, and Atonement has been made for one's sin. We get another view of this place prepared for us in Revelation 4:8-11, "And the four living creatures, each of them with six wings, are full of eyes all around and within, and day and night they never cease to say, Holy, holy, holy, is the Lord God Almighty, who was and is and is to come! And whenever the living creatures give glory and honor and thanks to him who is seated on the throne, who lives forever and ever, the twenty-four elders fall down before him who is seated on the throne and worship him who lives forever and ever. They cast their crowns before the throne, saying, Worthy are you, our Lord and God, to receive glory and honor and power, for you created all things, and by your will they existed and were created." The Chorus and Worship is endless as the Song of Adoration and Redemption echoes day and night throughout Heaven.

What must take place in our individual lives before we can have assurance that we will be admitted into God's Heaven? There are two Questions and Answers from the Westminster Shorter Catechism to consider - - - What is justification?

"Justification is an act of God's free grace, wherein he pardons all our sins, and accepts us as righteous in his sight, only for the righteousness of Christ imputed to us, and received by faith alone." We recall with Thanksgiving the words of Ephesians 1:7, "In whom we have redemption through his blood, the forgiveness of sins, according to the riches of his grace." Also, Romans 3:22-25, "Even the righteousness of God which is by faith of Jesus Christ unto all and upon all them that believe: for there is no difference: for all have sinned, and come short of the glory of God; being justified freely by his grace through the redemption that is in Christ Jesus: whom God hath set forth to be a propitiation through faith in his blood, to declare his righteousness for the remission of sins that are past, through the forbearance of God." The extent and impact of Justification having occurred in one's life is amplified by the definition from Easton's Bible Dictionary, namely, Justification "…is the judicial act of God, by which he pardons all the sins of those who believe in Christ, and accounts, accepts, and treats them as righteous in the eye of the law, i.e., as conformed to all its demands. In addition to the pardon of sin, justification declares that all the claims of the law are satisfied in respect of the justified. It is the act of a judge and not of a sovereign. The law is not relaxed or set aside, but is declared to be fulfilled in the strictest sense; and so the person justified is declared to be entitled to all the advantages and rewards arising from perfect obedience to the law…"

In keeping with the act of Justification, we must also understand the work of Sanctification. The Westminster Shorter Catechism asks: What Is Sanctification? The answer given: "Sanctification is the work of God's free grace, whereby we are renewed in the whole man after the image of God, and are enabled more and more to die unto sin, and live unto righteousness. Two of the supporting Scripture References are: II Thessalonians 2:13. "God hath from the beginning chosen you to salvation through sanctification of the Spirit and of the truth." And, Ephesians 4:23-24. "And be renewed in the spirit of your mind; and that ye put on the new man, which after God is created in righteousness and true holiness."

What is "True Holiness"?

Easton's Bible Dictionary defines Holiness: " in the highest sense belongs to God and to Christians as consecrated to God's service, and in so far as they are conformed in all things to the will of God. Personal holiness is a work of gradual development. It is carried on under many hindrances, hence the frequent admonitions to watchfulness, prayer, and perseverance."

We have an amplification of how the Bridegroom – Jesus Christ – desires His Bride – The Church – to be Prepared and Ready for

Him. To be in His Presence has as a minimum requirement stated in the Bride's description in Ephesians 5:21-33. The Bride – His Church - is to be:

1.   In Submission to the Lord
2.   Christ is The Head of The Church, His Body
3.   Christ is the Savior of and for The Body
4.   The Church is to submit to Christ in everything
5.   Christ loved the Church and gave Himself up for her
6.   That He might Sanctify her, having cleansed her by washing of water with The Word
7.   that he might present the church to himself in splendor, without spot or wrinkle or any such thing, that she might be holy and without blemish.
8.   Christ loves The Church and nourishes and cherishes it
9.   We are members of His Body
10. This mystery is profound, and I am saying that it refers to Christ and the church.

Jesus Christ wants His Church to be sanctified; cleansed by and through The Word; in splendor, without spot or wrinkle or any such thing, that she might be holy and without blemish.

It does us well to connect two concepts in terms of (1) The Church being "without spot or wrinkle or any such thing, that she might be holy and without blemish" and (2) the condition of the sacrificed being offered. Take as an example, the following passages of God's Word - - -

Romans 12:1 (ESV), "I appeal to you therefore, brothers, by the mercies of God, to present your bodies as a living sacrifice, holy and acceptable to God, which is your spiritual worship." The New Living Translation is: "And so, dear brothers and sisters, I plead with you to give your bodies to God. Let them be a living and holy sacrifice -- the kind he will accept. When you think of what

he has done for you, is this too much to ask?" Our bodies are to
be a living and holy sacrifice to God – the kind He will accept."
Ask yourself, what kind of sacrifice will He not accept? We gain
an insight by reading a graphic statement by the Lord in Malachi
1:6-14 - - "A son honors his father, and a servant his master. If
then I am a father, where is my honor? And if I am a master,
where is my fear? says the Lord of hosts to you, O priests, who
despise my name. But you say, How have we despised your
name? By offering polluted food upon my altar. But you say,
'How have we polluted you?' By saying that the Lord's table may
be despised. When you offer blind animals in sacrifice, is that not
evil? And when you offer those that are lame or sick, is that not
evil? Present that to your governor; will he accept you or show
you favor? says the Lord of hosts. And now entreat the favor of
God, that he may be gracious to us. With such a gift from your
hand, will he show favor to any of you? says the Lord of hosts.
Oh that there were one among you who would shut the doors, that
you might not kindle fire on my altar in vain! I have no pleasure
in you, says the Lord of hosts, and I will not accept an offering
from your hand. For from the rising of the sun to its setting my
name will be great among the nations, and in every place incense
will be offered to my name, and a pure offering. For my name
will be great among the nations, says the Lord of hosts. But you
profane it when you say that the Lord's table is polluted, and its
fruit, that is, its food may be despised. But you say, What a
weariness this is, and you snort at it, says the Lord of hosts. You
bring what has been taken by violence or is lame or sick, and this
you bring as your offering! Shall I accept that from your hand?
says the Lord. Cursed be the cheat who has a male in his flock,
and vows it, and yet sacrifices to the Lord what is blemished. For
I am a great King, says the Lord of hosts, and my name will be
feared among the nations."

The complaint of the Lord is reasoned and clear. They have
started bringing to Him less than what is required. They have

convinced themselves that no one will either notice or care. The Lord characterizes such insincere offerings as being "…what has been taken by violence or is lame or sick, and this you bring...Shall I accept that from your hand? says the Lord. Cursed be the cheat who has a male in his flock, and vows it, and yet sacrifices to the Lord what is blemished."

The Message Paraphrase is even more candid and specific – "You priests despise me! You say, Not so! How do we despise you? By your shoddy, sloppy, defiling worship. You ask, What do you mean, defiling? What's defiling about it? When you say, 'The altar of God is not important anymore; worship of God is no longer a priority, that's defiling. And when you offer worthless animals for sacrifices in worship, animals that you're trying to get rid of - blind and sick and crippled animals - isn't that defiling? Try a trick like that with your banker or your senator - how far do you think it will get you? God-of-the-Angel-Armies asks you. Get on your knees and pray that I will be gracious to you. You priests have gotten everyone in trouble. With this kind of conduct, do you think I'll pay attention to you? God-of-the-Angel-Armies asks you. Why doesn't one of you just shut the Temple doors and lock them? Then none of you can get in and play at religion with this silly, empty-headed worship. I am not pleased. The God-of-the-Angel-Armies is not pleased. And I don't want any more of this so-called worship! Offering God Something Hand-Me-Down, Broken, or Useless. I am honored all over the world. And there are people who know how to worship me all over the world, who honor me by bringing their best to me. They're saying it everywhere: God is greater, this God-of-the-Angel-Armies. All except you. Instead of honoring me, you profane me. You profane me when you say, Worship is not important, and what we bring to worship is of no account, and when you say, I'm bored - this doesn't do anything for me. You act so superior, sticking your noses in the air - act superior to me, God-of-the-Angel-Armies! And when you do offer something to me, it's a hand-me-down, or broken, or useless. Do you think I'm going to accept it? This is God speaking to you! A curse on the person who makes a big show of doing something great for me - an expensive sacrifice, say - and then at the last minute brings in something puny and worthless! I'm a great king, God-of-the-Angel-Armies, honored far and wide, and I'll not put up with it!"

John Wesley was known as a person focused on Holiness. Some random comments made by him are interesting to consider. (a) "Holiness is not flawlessness. A common misunderstanding is to think that holiness believers…think we can live without sin of any kind on this earth. The actual belief is that we can overcome by God's gracious gift the power of willful and habitual sin in our lives…The willful transgression of known laws can be overcome in the life of the believer by God's grace." (b) "In holiness doctrine the key role of the believer is surrender to the work of God. It is the surrender of the right to say no to God, and a request that God would give us the power to say yes… Increasing and deepening levels of surrender are what make the believer receptive to God's ongoing works of grace." (c) Holiness is not merely a private prayer closet faith. Call believers to community, to acts of service, to works of love, and to mutual support and activity. Weave practices of mercy and justice, ministry to the poor, hospitality to the stranger, and concern for orphans and widows into the practices and habits of the church's life in community. These practices fill life with love, reducing the room in life for selfishness, hatred, and greed."

John Wesley was teaching that Holiness will make a profound difference in an individual life, and through that transforming life, also have a practical impact on all types of people in all kinds of circumstances and situations. It is a personalizing of the Hymn by Philip P. Bliss - - -

More holiness give me, more strivings within.
More patience in suffering, more sorrow for sin.
More faith in my Savior, more sense of His care.
More joy in His service, more purpose in prayer.

More gratitude give me, more trust in the Lord.
More zeal for His glory, more hope in His Word.
More tears for His sorrows, more pain at His grief.
More meekness in trial, more praise for relief.

More purity give me, more strength to o'er come,
More freedom from earth-stains, more longings for home.
More fit for the kingdom, more useful I'd be,
More blessed and holy, more, Savior, like Thee.

Leviticus 11:44-45 establishes the standard for Holiness. We read: "I am the Lord your God. Consecrate yourselves therefore, and be holy, for I am holy. You shall not defile yourselves with any swarming thing that crawls on the ground. For I am the Lord who brought you up out of the land of Egypt to be your God. You shall therefore be holy, for I am holy."

And lest one thinks that this standard no longer applies, the Apostle Peter wrote in I Peter 1:14-19, "As obedient children, do not be conformed to the passions of your former ignorance, but as he who called you is holy, you also be holy in all your conduct, since it is written, You shall be holy, for I am holy. And if you call on him as Father who judges impartially according to each one's deeds, conduct yourselves with fear throughout the time of your exile, knowing that you were ransomed from the futile ways inherited from your forefathers, not with perishable things such as silver or gold, but with the precious blood of Christ, like that of a lamb without blemish or spot." Peter is emphasizing that as those who are redeemed and who been ransomed, there is an obligation to be Holy because the Lord who ransomed and redeemed you is

Holy. There is no shortcut to Holiness. Holiness requires full commitment and faithful obedience to God and His Word and His Standard.

The Sanctification not only means one is to be Holy as God is Holy, but it also involves Perfection – you shall be Perfect as your Father in Heaven is Perfect. The passage that focuses on Perfection is Matthew 5:43-48, "You have heard that it was said, You shall love your neighbor and hate your enemy. But I say to you, Love your enemies and pray for those who persecute you, so that you may be sons of your Father who is in heaven. For he makes his sun rise on the evil and on the good, and sends rain on the just and on the unjust. For if you love those who love you, what reward do you have? Do not even the tax collectors do the same? And if you greet only your brothers, what more are you doing than others? Do not even the Gentiles do the same? You therefore must be perfect, as your heavenly Father is perfect." The Lord gives a very basic summary of The Law when He states in Luke 19:25-28, "And behold, a lawyer stood up to put him to the test, saying, Teacher, what shall I do to inherit eternal life? He said to him, What is written in the Law? How do you read it? And he answered, You shall love the Lord your God with all your heart and with all your soul and with all your strength and with all your mind, and your neighbor as yourself. And he said to him, You have answered correctly; do this, and you will live."

Jesus is speaking about agape love – the same love God had when He so loved the world, and gave us His Son. In Matthew 5, Jesus expands that agape love, not just to one's neighbor, but also to one's enemies. It is a love that flows out of forgiveness, mercy and grace.

When Jesus Christ mandates that one move on to Perfection, it causes one to wonder when and where that can be achieved and attained. Can I be perfect during this lifetime? Is Perfection that which all true followers of Christ realize when they are united to Him in Heaven? Peter shares some helpful thoughts when he writes in - I Peter 1:3-5 - - -

Blessed be the God and Father of our Lord Jesus Christ! According to his great mercy, he has caused us to be born again to a living hope through the resurrection of Jesus Christ from the dead, to an inheritance that is imperishable, undefiled, and unfading, kept in heaven for you, who by God's power are being guarded through faith for a salvation ready to be revealed in the last time."

The inheritance we have received is imperishable, undefiled and unfading. It is kept in Heaven for us who are being guarded by God's power... In his second Epistle, Peter continues...

II Peter 1:3-10
"His divine power has granted to us all things that pertain to life and godliness, through the knowledge of him who called us to his own glory and excellence, by which he has granted to us his precious and very great promises, so that through them you may become partakers of the divine nature, having escaped from the corruption that is in the world because of sinful desire. For this very reason, make every effort to supplement your faith with virtue... knowledge... self-control... steadfastness... godliness... brotherly affection... love. For if these qualities are yours and are increasing, they keep you from being ineffective or unfruitful in the knowledge of our Lord Jesus Christ. For whoever lacks these qualities is so nearsighted that he is blind, having forgotten that he was cleansed from his former sins. Therefore, brothers, be all the more diligent to make your calling and election sure, for if you practice these qualities you will never fall."

We need to note - - -

(a)   His Divine Power has enabled us to escape from the
        corruption that is in the world because of the sinful de-
        sire…

(b)   His Divine Power has also granted us qualities that can
        keep us from being ineffective and unfruitful.

(c)   We are assured that if we Practice these Qualities, we will
        never fall or fail.

Hebrews 6:1 reminds us: "Therefore let us leave the elementary
doctrine of Christ and go on to maturity, not laying again a
foundation of repentance from dead works and of faith toward
God." A simplistic thought is that this is the process where one
moves from the "elementary" – Jesus Loves Me, This I Know –
to the more mature level of – My Jesus, I Love Thee, I Know
Thou Art Mine. The word translated "maturity" in the ESV and
the NIV is properly translated in the NKJV as "perfection." It's
an instruction that's urging one to Grow Up in the Lord. It intends
that we be experiencing inward righteousness and holiness, with a
sense that we are moving closer into the presence of God and
knowing Him more intimately. It also means one is growing in a
desire for God and His controlling more and more of one's life.

No one will know total and complete perfection in this lifetime –
but one can come closer and closer to it by practicing the presence of God in one's life. Then - at the moment when one passes
from this world and life – and – crosses into eternity, it will be
crossing over the threshold into full and complete perfection in
the presence of Jesus Christ forever.

Personal Study Questions - - -

On a scale of one to ten (one being lowest and ten being highest), where would you score yourself in terms of your sanctification?

On that same scale, how important do you personally believe Sanctification is for your life?

Have you ever made a choice to offer the Lord less than what he requires in terms of your time, talent and finances?

How do you think The Lord views the responses you have given to these questions?

What one place in your life do you believe requires immediate attention by you?

Imitators or Imitations

In Matthew's Gospel, the Lord Jesus Christ extends calls for commitment. When He issues that call, He also asserts what He will do with and for the one responding to Him. It is a case of "if you respond – I will reward." It is all part of the process of one knowing God more intimately. It will involve commitment and entail obedience. There will be a positive response and a readiness to sacrifice. Without it, one can never come to the point of knowing God.

In 1972, Dr. J. I. Packer wrote a book entitled: Knowing God. A brief summary of his goal and purpose for his tome can be summarized from points gleaned from his book.

Five Truths about God

There are five basic truths, five foundational principles that will form the foundation of one's study of God.

1) God has spoken to man, and the Bible is his Word, given to us to make us wise unto salvation.
2) God is Lord and King over this world; he rules all things for his own glory, displaying his perfections in all that he does, in order that men and angels may worship and adore him.
3) God is Savior, active in sovereign love through the Lord Jesus Christ to rescue believers from the guilt and power of sin, to adopt them as his children and to bless them accordingly.
4) God is triune; there are within the Godhead three persons, the Father, the Son, and the Holy Spirit; and the work of salvation is one in which all three act together, the Father

purposing redemption, the Son securing it and the Spirit applying it.

5)   Godliness means responding to God's revelation in trust and obedience, faith and worship, prayer and praise, submission and service. Life must be seen and lived in the light of God's Word. This, and nothing else, is true religion.

Dr. Packer states Evidences of Knowing God based upon a study of the Book and Life of Daniel:

1.   "Those who know God have great energy for God. In one of the prophetic chapters of Daniel we read, the people that do know their God shall be strong, and do exploits (11:32 KJV). RSV renders thus: the people who know their God shall stand firm and take action."

2.   "Those who know God have great thoughts of God. . . .there is, perhaps, no more vivid or sustained presentation of the many sided reality of God's sovereignty in the whole Bible [than Daniel]. In the face of the might and splendor of the Babylonian empire which had swallowed up Palestine and the prospect of further great world empires to follow, dwarfing Israel by every standard of human calculation, the book as a whole forms a dramatic reminder that the God of Israel is King of kings and Lord of lords, "that Heaven rules" (4:26), that God's hand is on history at every point, that history, indeed, is no more than "his story," the unfolding of his eternal plan, and that the kingdom which will triumph in the end is God's."

3.   "Those who know God show great boldness for God. Daniel and his friends were men who stuck their necks out. This was not foolhardiness. They knew what the were doing. They had counted the cost. They had measured the

risk. They were well aware what the outcome of their actions would be unless God miraculously intervened, as in fact he did. But these things did not move them. Once they were convinced that their stand was right, and that loyalty to their God required them to take it, then, in Oswald Chambers's phrase, they, "smilingly washed their hands of the consequences." "We must obey God rather than men!" said the apostles (Acts 5:39). "Neither count I my life dear to myself, so that I might finish my course with joy," said Paul (Acts 20:24)."

4.   "Those who know God have great contentment in God. There is no peace like the peace of those whose minds are possessed with full assurance that they have known God, and God has know them, and that this relationship guarantees God's favor to them in life, through death and on for ever. This is the peace of which Paul speaks in Romans 5:1, "since we have been justified through faith, we have peace with God through our Lord Jesus Christ"— and whose substance he analyzes in full in Romans 8. "There is now no condemnation for those who are in Christ Jesus...The Spirit himself testifies with our spirit that we are God's children... heirs of God...We know that in all things God works for the good of those who love him...Those he justified, he also glorified...If God is for us, who can be against us? ...Who will bring any charge against those who God has chosen? ...Who shall separate us from the love of Christ?...I am convince that neither death nor life...neither the present nor the future...will be able to separate us from the love of God that is in Christ Jesus or Lord" (vv.1, 16–17, 28, 30, 31, 33, 35, 38–39)."

Perhaps the above will whet your appetite to secure a copy of Knowing God by Dr. J. I. Packer. This book is still available from several internet book sellers.

In order for one to begin to Know God, one has to be attentive in order to hear God's Call, and to have a readiness to respond when the Master says – "Come!"

Two of the meaningful examples of Christ's particular call are significant - - -

1) Matthew 4:18-22
"While walking by the Sea of Galilee, he saw two brothers, Simon (who is called Peter) and Andrew his brother, casting a net into the sea, for they were fishermen. And he said to them, Follow me, and I will make you fishers of men. Immediately they left their nets and followed him. And going on from there he saw two other brothers, James the son of Zebedee and John his brother, in the boat with Zebedee their father, mending their nets, and he called them. Immediately they left the boat and their father and followed him."

2)   Matthew 10:27-30
"All things have been handed over to me by my Father, and no one knows the Son except the Father, and no one knows the Father except the Son and anyone to whom the Son chooses to reveal him. Come to me, all who labor and are heavy laden, and I will give you rest. Take my yoke upon you, and learn from me, for I am gentle and lowly in heart, and you will find rest for your souls. For my yoke is easy, and my burden is light."

No one can be an imitator of Christ until he Comes to Jesus Christ, begins to Follow Him, and is totally engaged and desirous of Knowing Him. Granted, there are different imitations that can mesmerize others and convince many that they are real – but they are fakes – imitations.

An example of this is given in II Thessalonians 2:8-12, "The coming of the lawless one is by the activity of Satan with all power and false signs and wonders, and with all wicked deception for those who are perishing, because they refused to love the truth and so be saved. Therefore God sends them a strong delusion, so that they may believe what is false, in order that all may be condemned who did not believe the truth but had pleasure in unrighteousness." Do you understand the significant statement being made? It is, "the activity of Satan with all power and false signs and wonders, and with all wicked deception for those who are perishing," It looks good and is appealing – but – it is false and an imitation.

This is similar to the words of Jesus in Matthew 7:21-23, "Not everyone who says to me, Lord, Lord, will enter the kingdom of heaven, but the one who does the will of my Father who is in heaven. On that day many will say to me, Lord, Lord, did we not prophesy in your name, and cast out demons in your name, and do many mighty works in your name? And then will I declare to them, I never knew you; depart from me, you workers of lawlessness." It is clear that Jesus repudiates religious activity being substituted for knowing and following Him. Jesus allows that there will be those who will rest upon the activities of "prophesy, casting out demons, and doing mighty works" – even claiming to do them in the name of Jesus Christ. Their problem is that they did not know Jesus Christ intimately and they were not imitators of Him. They were imitations who were pretending to be the real thing.

A distinction must be made between one who is an Imitator of Christ and one who has merely become an imitation. It is just like rare jewels, such as a diamond. A True Diamond will have a certain color and hardness that distinguish it from other stones. Zircon has been common as a Diamond Substitute and has the characteristics and qualities that give an appearance of being a real diamond. The untrained eye may believe it is a costly stone, whereas the trained eye will immediately know that it is not a valuable diamond at all but a skillful imitation resembling the real stone.

There are several enjoinders in Scripture that mandate one should be an Imitator and not an Imitation. Consider just a few of these references - - - Hebrews 6:10-12 - "For God is not unjust so as to overlook your work and the love that you have shown for his name in serving the saints, as you still do. And we desire each one of you to show the same earnestness to have the full assurance of hope until the end, so that you may not be sluggish, but imitators of those who through faith and patience inherit the promises." There are those who model faith and patience. You are to make the choice to imitate them, and with them, inherit the promises.

Ephesians 5:1-2 - Therefore be imitators of God, as beloved children. And walk in love, as Christ loved us and gave himself up for us, a fragrant offering and sacrifice to God." The one who is an Imitator will walk in love as Christ loved, and to live in such a way that the words, thoughts and actions will be a fragrant offering and sacrifice to God.

I Thessalonians 2:13-15 - "And we also thank God constantly for this, that when you received the word of God, which you heard from us, you accepted it not as the word of men but as what it really is, the word of God, which is at work in you believers. For you ...became imitators of the churches of God in Christ Jesus that are in Judea. For you suffered the same things from your own countrymen as they did from the Jews, who killed both the Lord Jesus and the prophets, and drove us out, and displease God and oppose all mankind." This is a case where the one who is an Imitator will take a stand with those of like precious faith. There is a willingness to identify with those who accept and embrace God's truth regardless of any personal cost or persecution. It is based solidly upon the Word of God which is at work in fellow-believers – these are worthy of being Imitated.

There are some interesting warnings and denunciations given about those who have proven to be imitations, untrustworthy and phonies. For instance, you will find this in Romans 16:17-20, where Paul notes and writes: "I appeal to you, brothers, to watch out for those who cause divisions and create obstacles contrary to the doctrine that you have been taught; avoid them. For such persons do not serve our Lord Christ, but their own appetites, and by smooth talk and flattery they deceive the hearts of the naive. For your obedience is known to all, so that I rejoice over you, but I want you to be wise as to what is good and innocent as to what is evil. The God of peace will soon crush Satan under your feet. The grace of our Lord Jesus Christ be with you." Note the characteristics of the Imitations - - -

- They cause divisions
- They create obstacles
- They do not serve the Lord Christ but their own appetites
- They employ smooth talk and flattery
- They deceive the hearts of the naïve

The warning he gives is - - -

- Watch out those who are Imitations
- Avoid them.

In II Timothy 4:9-16, Paul gives these personal instructions to Timothy and singles out those who have proven to be Imitations: "Do your best to come to me soon. For Demas, in love with this present world, has deserted me...Alexander the coppersmith did me great harm; the Lord will repay him according to his deeds. Beware of him yourself, for he strongly opposed our message. At my first defense no one came to stand by me, but all deserted me…but the Lord stood by me and strengthened me, so that through me the message might be fully proclaimed and all the Gentiles might hear it. So I was rescued from the lion's mouth…" About the Imitations who surfaced, he wrote - - -

- Demas, in love with this present world, is a deserter
- Alexander the Coppersmith did me great harm – he is opposed to
- The Message we preached and taught
- Others whom he equates as "the lion's mouth"

Just as an aside, the reference to the lion's mouth, this may be an allusion to Hebrews 11:32-34, "And what more shall I say? For time would fail me to tell of…those…who through faith conquered kingdoms, enforced justice, obtained promises, stopped the mouths of lions, quenched the power of fire, escaped the edge of the sword, were made strong out of weakness, became mighty in war, put foreign armies to flight…" At any rate, there was then as there is now, Imitations who will ultimately cause harm where they can and undermine the Gospel ministry if they could. This may be one reason Jesus said to His disciples, "Be as wise as serpents and as harmless as doves."

Others are singled out in Scripture as being among those who were Imitations. Joshua 7 gives considerable detail about Achan who succumbed to personal desire and greed; who yielded to the temptation to take what was not his to have; buried it in his tent so he could pretend that he was one of the group and had done nothing wrong – except and until – the anger of The Lord burned against all the people of Israel. Because of one man's sin, all of the people were suffering loss, shame and humiliation. The moment of accountability approaches! It will always come! As the Imitation – Achan – stands before Joshua, he confesses what he has done. In Joshua 7:24-25, we read what then occurs: "And Joshua and all Israel with him took Achan… and the silver and the cloak and the bar of gold, and his sons and daughters and his oxen and donkeys and sheep and his tent and all that he had. And they brought them up to the Valley of Achor. And Joshua said, Why did you bring trouble on us? The Lord brings trouble on you today. And all Israel stoned him with stones. They burned them with fire and stoned them with stones."

Another Imitation is mentioned in Acts 5:1-11. Ananias and Sapphira allowed themselves to be Imitations. They wanted to be accepted by the group but deceit and selfishness ruled in their lives. The text states that they: "sold a piece of property, and with his wife's knowledge he kept back for himself some of the proceeds and brought only a part of it and laid it at the apostles' feet. But Peter said, Ananias, why has Satan filled your heart to lie to the Holy Spirit and to keep back for yourself part of the proceeds of the land?" Note the indictment - - -

- He connived with his wife to misrepresent what they had received for the sold land
- Peter confronts him: Why has Satan filled your heart to lie to the Holy Spirit?
- Why did you decide "to keep back for yourself part of the proceeds of the land?"

Because of his egregious act, verse 5 states: "When Ananias heard these words, he fell down and breathed his last. And great fear came upon all who heard of it."

The plot now thickens. "After an interval of about three hours his wife came in, not knowing what had happened. And Peter said to her, Tell me whether you sold the land for so much. And she said, Yes, for so much." The web of deception is revealed and the her sin is also exposed. Sapphira has allowed herself to become an Imitation as well. Her indictment and judgment is identical to that of her husband. In verse 9, "Peter said to her, How is it that you have agreed together to test the Spirit of the Lord? Behold, the feet of those who have buried your husband are at the door, and they will carry you out. Immediately she fell down at his feet and breathed her last...And great fear came upon the whole church and upon all who heard of these things." Imitations if left unchecked, will always seek to distract and detract from the work of the Lord. The Imitations need to be purged – just as Achan was removed from the camp of God's people in Joshua 7, and as Ananias and Sapphira were removed from the Church in Acts 5. Drastic action? Yes! Sin is a serious matter and requires confrontation and remedy. In the modern culture, many times the Achan types are allowed to be deacons in the Church, sometimes even Sunday School Teachers. There is also the possibility of the Ananias types becoming Elders in the Church, and the Sapphira types becoming Circle Leaders or Children Workers. The Imitations need to be removed from Leadership positions and places of influence in The Church of the Lord Jesus Christ. If you're tempted to think such things are non-consequential, you should read Revelation 2 and 3 and note the fact regarding – "The words of him who holds the seven stars in his right hand, who walks among the seven golden lamp-stands..." Note the recurring words: "I know..."

Personal Study Questions - - -

When you look into your spiritual mirror – the Word of God – do you see yourself as an Imitator or an Imitation? Why?

What thoughts, words or deeds in your life – when weighed before the Lord – are real? Which ones are imitations? What do you think you should do about it? When?

Do you believe God is as angry today with the sin of theft in the camp and deceit in The Church? Should it be confronted and dealt with as it was in Joshua 7 and Acts 5? Why- or – Why not?

If someone Imitated you, would it bring them closed to Christ?

Consider: I Corinthians 11:1

"Be imitators of me, as I am of Christ."

Could you use these words with another – Be an imitator of me, as I am of Christ? Should you be able to do so?

Seeking and Finding

When did this premise of "seeking and finding" enter into the sphere of life? What actuated it? What circumstance provoked it? Where was it first promulgated?

In Genesis 3:8-11, there is the first indication that something dramatic has occurred in The Creation of God. Man (Adam) had been created in innocence, as was Woman (Eve). They knew the reality of walking in the presence of God every day – in the cool of the evening. It was a time of sweet fellowship. But then – something changed all of that forever. One evening, The Creator comes for this established time of fellowship and communion – but Man (Adam) and Woman (Eve) were not at the appointed place at the appointed time. Why? Had they not completed their daily chores? Had they been so preoccupied that the appointed meeting time sneaked up on them? Had they become weary or bored with these daily meetings? What had changed? What happened? The text includes this description: "And they heard the sound of the Lord God walking in the garden in the cool of the day, and the man and his wife hid themselves from the presence of the Lord God among the trees of the garden. But the Lord God called to the man and said to him, Where are you? And he said, I heard the sound of you in the garden, and I was afraid, because I was naked, and I hid myself. He said, Who told you that you were naked? Have you eaten of the tree of which I commanded you not to eat?" What a dynamic moment! Adam and Eve hiding themselves from the presence of God; God seeking them and calling to them; man responding feebly about nakedness; and the probing question of Almighty God - :Who told you that you were naked? This is followed quickly by a second question: "Have you eaten of the tree of which I commanded you not to eat?" Did they do what they had been told not to do? How will this moment of truth and confrontation be handled? Will it be a contrite admission? What can and will be said at such an obvious guilt-moment?

In Genesis 3:12-13, the response of Adam and Eve is given: " The man said, The woman whom you gave to be with me, she gave me fruit of the tree, and I ate. Then the Lord God said to the woman, What is this that you have done? The woman said, The serpent deceived me, and I ate." This act was the beginning of the "blame-game." Adam said to the Lord: "It was Eve - the Woman you created from my rib – the one You gave me, the one you thought I needed and could not do without – that Woman gave me a piece of that delicious fruit and I ate it." Eve said to the Lord: "It was the serpent that You created – that beautiful and subtle reptile – he convinced me that it would be alright and there would be no negative response from you if it was taken and ingested." Besides, the serpent also allowed that we would know You better because we would be just like You! The appeal we were presented and pondered was: "For God knows that when you eat of it your eyes will be opened, and you will be like God, knowing good and evil." But – but – all we noticed and realized was that we were naked, and fearful – so afraid now - and when we heard You coming and calling – we tried to hide from You. They would soon realize there would be greater consequences – penalties they had never considered or imagined – would become part of their existence. Furthermore, it would also affect all of their offspring – their descendants. The summary of this is stated in Romans 5:12-21 (Selected), "Therefore, just as sin came into the world through one man, and death through sin, and so death spread to all men because all sinned - for sin indeed was in the world before the law was given, but sin is not counted where there is no law. Yet death reigned from Adam to Moses, even over those whose sinning was not like the transgression of Adam, who was a type of the one who was to come…as one trespass led to condemnation for all men…For as by the one man's disobedience the many were made sinners…" Long before this incident took place in time, God had set in motion a plan that would provide redemption for disobedience. The indication of a redemptive plan is first shared in Genesis 3:14-15, we have the Prolegomena – the first indication of the Gospel and Redemption: "The Lord God said to the serpent, Because you have done this, cursed are you above all livestock and above all beasts of the field; on your belly you shall go, and dust you shall eat all the days of your life. I will put enmity between you and the woman, and between your offspring and her offspring; he shall bruise your head, and you shall bruise his heel."

In terms of the Counsels of God, a determinative Covenant of Redemption was already in place before The Creation. This is stated in I Peter 1:18-20 (NIV): "For you know that it was not with perishable things such as silver or gold that you were redeemed from the empty way of life handed down to you from your forefathers, but with the precious blood of Christ, a lamb without blemish or defect. He was chosen before the creation of the world, but was revealed in these last times for your sake." The New Living Translation states: "For you know that God paid a ransom to save you from the empty life you inherited from your ancestors. And the ransom he paid was not mere gold or silver. He paid for you with the precious lifeblood of Christ, the sinless, spotless Lamb of God. God chose him for this purpose long before the world began, but now in these final days, he was sent to the earth for all to see. And he did this for you." The beauty in God's Redemptive Plan is that Almighty God, the Creator of the Universe, continues to seek, call out to, finds us wherever we are, and gives us the opportunity to be saved from the wrath to come.

This is clearly stated by the Lord Jesus Christ when in Luke 19:9-10 when He visited with Zacchaeus, "And Jesus said to him, Today salvation has come to this house, since he also is a son of Abraham. For the Son of Man came to seek and to save the lost." He will seek - - find - - save - - today.

No one should assume a posture of attempting to hide from God. There ought to be a growing desire – fanned into a flame and with increasing heat – as one seeks for the Lord relentlessly until The Lord is found. The words in Scripture "But God" are so meaningful – Ephesians 2:4-5 – "But God, being rich in mercy, because of the great love with which he loved us, 5 even when we were dead in our trespasses, made us alive together with Christ--by grace you have been saved." By His mercy - He continues to seek us, call us by name, relentless until we are found by Him – and then – saves us - by grace we have been found – by grace we have been saved.

Is it any wonder that John Newton penned the words to Amazing Grace that are a favorite and testimony of many?

1.   Amazing grace! How sweet the sound
        That saved a wretch like me!
        I once was lost, but now am found;
        Was blind, but now I see.

2.   'Twas grace that taught my heart to fear,
        And grace my fears relieved;
        How precious did that grace appear
        The hour I first believed!

3.   Through many dangers, toils and snares,
        I have already come;
        'Tis grace hath brought me safe thus far,
        And grace will lead me home.

There are many Scriptures that teach us both the necessity and benefit as one seeks the Lord.

Jeremiah 29:13-14 - "You will seek me and find me, when you seek me with all your heart. I will be found by you, declares the Lord…"

Psalm 27:8-14 (selected) - "You have said, Seek my face. My heart says to you, Your face, Lord, do I seek. Hide not your face from me. Turn not your servant away in anger, O you who have been my help. Cast me not off; forsake me not, O God of my salvation…Teach me your way, O Lord, and lead me on a level path…I believe that I shall look upon the goodness of the Lord in the land of the living! Wait for the Lord; be strong, and let your heart take courage; wait for the Lord!

Isaiah 55:6-8 - "Seek the Lord while he may be found; call upon him while he is near; let the wicked forsake his way, and the unrighteous man his thoughts; let him return to the Lord, that he may have compassion on him, and to our God, for he will abundantly pardon. For my thoughts are not your thoughts, neither are your ways my ways, declares the Lord."

The other part to this appeal to seek the Lord while He may be found, is given in the form of two questions found in Mark 8:34-37, "And calling the crowd to him with his disciples, he said to them, If anyone would come after me, let him deny himself and take up his cross and follow me. For whoever would save his life will lose it, but whoever loses his life for my sake and the gospel's will save it. For what does it profit a man to gain the whole world and forfeit his soul? For what can a man give in return for his soul?" The questions are:

- What does it profit a man to gain the whole world and forfeit his soul?
- What can a man give in return for his soul?

The only response to both questions is a resounding "Nothing!"

There are many people in the world today who are material-minded rather than spiritual-minded. Many of them do not even pause to think upon spiritual verities. It appears to be all business all of the time. That's the plight of the secular man.

Sometimes it is difficult to persevere in "Seeking", and challenges along the way are often formidable. Two of the characters in The Pilgrim's Progress demonstrate how easily one can be dissuaded from pressing forward. One of them is Pliable - A neighbor of Christian's who accompanies him for a while. After falling in the Slough of Despond, Pliable is discouraged and returns home, only to be mocked by the townsfolk. The other is Worldly Wiseman - A reasonable and practical man whom Christian encounters early in his journey. Worldly Wiseman tries unsuccessfully to urge Christian to give up his religious foolishness and live a contented secular life. So it is today – too pliable; too worldly minded; too busy; too uninterested; too unconcerned; always an excuse; possessing the rationale that there's plenty of time yet.

Psalm 63:1-3 finds David speaking about a specific time and place in His life where a spiritual exercise must take place. He doesn't believe he can survive if it is neglected by him. Note how he expresses his inner thoughts and desires: "O God, you are my God; earnestly I seek you; my soul thirsts for you; my flesh faints for you, as in a dry and weary land where there is no water. So I have looked upon you in the sanctuary, beholding your power and glory. Because your steadfast love is better than life, my lips will praise you." A phrase used in the ESV – "earnestly I seek You" is expressed in the NKJV as – "early will I seek You." The thirsty and hungering soul will do that – seek the Lord early, earnestly and often.

Max Lucado writes so brilliantly and giftedly. He comments on Mark 7:31-35. "Quite a passage, isn't it? Jesus is presented with a man who is deaf and has a speech impediment. Perhaps he stammered. Maybe he spoke with a lisp. Perhaps, because of his deafness, he never learned to articulate words properly.

"Jesus, refusing to exploit the situation, took the man aside. He looked him in the face. Knowing it would be useless to talk, he explained what he was about to do through gestures. He spat and touched the man's tongue, telling him that whatever restricted his speech was about to be removed. He touched his ears. They, for the first time, were about to hear. But before the man said a word or heard a sound, Jesus did something I never would have anticipated.

"He sighed.

"I might have expected a clap or a song or a prayer. Even a "Hallelujah!" or a brief lesson might have been appropriate. But the Son of God did none of these.

"Instead, he paused, looked into heaven, and sighed.

"From the depths of his being came a rush of emotion that said more than words.

"Sigh.

"The word seemed out of place. I'd never thought of God as one who sighs.

"I'd thought of God as one who commands. I'd thought of God as one who weeps. I'd thought of God as one who called forth the dead with a command or created the universe with a word…but a God who sighs?"

What does the word "sigh" mean? A sigh means: "to let out one's breath audibly, as from sorrow, weariness, or relief; to yearn or long; pine."

Did Jesus "sigh" because of the great compassion he inwardly felt toward the one who had suffered so long? Did Jesus "sigh" because of the unbelief of those who observed Him? Did He "sigh" because the Disciples were apprehensive about what their Master was doing? Did He "sigh" because the man He reached out to was content with how he'd always been? Did He "sigh" because He knew this would be another miracle ignored and soon forgotten?

There are reassuring words for the seeking soul in Deuteronomy 4:29-31, "But from there you will seek the Lord your God and you will find him, if you search after him with all your heart and with all your soul. When you are in tribulation, and all these things come upon you in the latter days, you will return to the Lord your God and obey his voice. For the Lord your God is a merciful God. He will not leave you or destroy you or forget the covenant with your fathers that he swore to them."

Some contemporary music contains helpful and very useful words for personal worship of The Lord. One of the Choruses that does this is:

I will sing of the mercies of the Lord forever
I will sing, I will sing.
I will sing of the mercies of the Lord forever,
I will sing of the mercies of the Lord.
With my mouth will I make known
Thy faithfulness, Thy faithfulness.
With my mouth will I make known
Thy faithfulness to all generations...

This is the song of the redeemed – the forgiven – who have believed and received the mercy of God in their behalf. Such an act of God, instills music in the heart of the one who has benefitted from His love, mercy and grace. It demonstrates that if you seek Him and find Him, you will soon learn that He has been seeking you all along and you have been found by Him.

Personal Study Questions - - -

If living in the presence of God is vital, how often do you seek Him? How often do you commune with Him?

When was the last time the Lord has spoken to you in the quiet moments you spend with Him? What did He say that was timely and significant for you?

Does God "sigh" because of you – or – might He respond with a "Good Morning! I've been waiting for you!"?

When was the last time you privately sang to (with) the Lord? What song did you sing?

Basics for Living in God's Presence

PSALM 16:5-8

"Lord, you have assigned me my portion and my cup; you have made my lot secure. The boundary lines have fallen for me in pleasant places; surely I have a delightful inheritance. I will praise the Lord, who counsels me; even at night my heart instructs me. I have set the Lord always before me. Because he is at my right hand, I will not be shaken."

In the day and time in which we live, how should we approach God? Is He relevant to the times in which we live? Is He foremost in our thinking and lifestyle? Do we believe He cares about us and this world enough to intervene in the affairs of men and nations? Does God really know what is going on?

How we approach God is vital. Our thoughts about God should include His Creation and Power. Perhaps that would include some thought about His vastness and greatness – maybe His attributes would come to mind, as well. The Westminster Shorter Catechism Number 4 Asks and Answers – What is God? "God is a Spirit, infinite, eternal, and unchangeable, in his being, wisdom, power, holiness, justice, goodness, and truth." We need to comprehend God and His Attributes. Those Attributes that are noncommunicable are - -

- His Eternity – God is from everlasting to everlasting
- His Omnipresence – God is everywhere present all the time
- His Omniscience - God knows all things in detail at all times

- His Omnipotence - God is all-powerful and able to do all things at anytime
- His Immutability - God is unchangeable in all his ways in all generations.

Is this your God – the one you Worship and to Whom you pray? In your mind and belief-system, is He the One Who is more than sufficient, and able to do immeasurably more than you can ask or imagine? Consider how the Psalmist David thought about God – Psalm 139:1-11 – "O Lord, you have searched me and you know me. You know when I sit and when I rise; you perceive my thoughts from afar. You discern my going out and my lying down; you are familiar with all my ways. Before a word is on my tongue you know it completely, O Lord. You hem me in--behind and before; you have laid your hand upon me. Such knowledge is too wonderful for me, too lofty for me to attain. Where can I go from your Spirit? Where can I flee from your presence? If I go up to the heavens, you are there; if I make my bed in the depths, you are there. If I rise on the wings of the dawn, if I settle on the far side of the sea, even there your hand will guide me, your right hand will hold me fast. If I say, Surely the darkness will hide me and the light become night around me, even the darkness will not be dark to you; the night will shine like the day, for darkness is as light to you…"

We read about another individual who came to a similar aware-ness about God – albeit in very rare circumstances – in Jonah 2:1-7 – "From inside the fish Jonah prayed to the Lord his God. He said: "In my distress I called to the Lord, and he answered me. From the depths of the grave I called for help, and you listened to my cry. You hurled me into the deep, into the very heart of the seas, and the currents swirled about me; all your waves and breakers swept over me. I said, 'I have been banished from your sight; yet I will look again toward your holy temple. The engulf-ing waters threatened me, and the deep surrounded me; seaweed was wrapped around my head. To the roots of the mountains I sank down; the earth beneath barred me in forever. But you brought my life up from the pit, O Lord my God. When my life was ebbing away, I remembered you, Lord, and my prayer rose to you…" This was a means God used to gain the attention of Jonah and to make him willing to do that which God wanted him to do. Drastic? Yes! Sometimes it takes the "drastic" in our lives as well. Why is it that way? As we live in challenging times with overwhelming uncertainties and insurmountable unknowns, we fail at times to contemplate and realize that our God is Omniscient – He knows and He cares.

If one desires to live in the presence of God, you need to know Who He is and what you should know about Him. Moreover, you will begin to learn what He knows about you, and what His expectations are for your life as one of His very own.

While this chapter is not a detailed study about God, there are other qualities, characteristics and attributes that you will learn from and about Him as you live in His presence - - -

- The decrees of God – The Shorter Catechism Number 7 answers: "The decrees of God are, his eternal purpose, according to the counsel of his will, whereby, for his own glory, he hath foreordained whatsoever comes to pass."

This means one will begin to learn more about and gain an understanding regarding - - -

- The knowledge of God
- The foreknowledge of God
- The sovereignty of God
- The holiness of God

As one grows in this relationship of living in the presence of God, there will be increased awareness about - The faithfulness of God; The goodness of God; The patience of God; The grace of God; The mercy of God; The love of God; The wrath of God; The will of God; and – The plan that He has for your life. Our tendency can allow us to think about God in the abstract – someone who is remote and far away. We need to – and – should want to – implement Deuteronomy 4:29 – "But if from there you seek the Lord your God, you will find him if you look for him with all your heart and with all your soul." The "there" of this verse can be the "anywhere" you find yourself. That would be your "there", and from your "there", "if…you seek the Lord your God, you will find him if you look for him with all your heart and with all your soul."

And from our "there", we will also learn and want to know the reality of - Matthew 7:7-8 – If from "there" you "Ask - it will be given to you; seek - you will find; knock - the door will be opened to you. For everyone who asks receives; he who seeks finds; and to him who knocks, the door will be opened." You will also learn the bountifulness of God's response to the one who asks, seeks and knocks – Luke 6:38 – "…it will be given to you. A good measure, pressed down, shaken together and running over, will be poured into your lap…"

We will want to live Biblically and in close relationship with the Lord and to heed His Word. Words such as - I Chronicles 28:9 – "And you, my son Solomon, acknowledge the God of your father, and serve him with wholehearted devotion and with a willing mind, for the Lord searches every heart and understands every motive behind the thoughts. If you seek him, he will be found by you; but if you forsake him, he will reject you forever." There is an enlarging responsibility for the one making the commitment to live daily in the presence of God. It will cause one to gain further insight and assurance – Psalm 9:10 – "Those who know your name will trust in you, for you, LORD, have never forsaken those who seek you." – and – Psalm 14:2, "The LORD looks down from heaven on the sons of men to see if there are any who understand, any who seek God." There is the enjoinder of Zephaniah 2:3, "Seek the LORD, all you humble of the land, you who do what he commands. Seek righteousness, seek humility; perhaps you will be sheltered on the day of the LORD'S anger." For those who seek Him with all their heart, soul, strength and mind – they will be sheltered and protected by The Lord.

It does us well to remember the contemporary Worship Chorus:

> In His Presence, There Is Comfort,
> In His Presence, There Is Peace.
> When We Seek The Father's Heart,
> We Will Find Such Blessed Assurance,
> In The Presence Of The Lord.

The second stanza changes slightly and personalizes the words…

> In YOUR Presence, There Is Comfort,
> In YOUR Presence, There Is Peace.
> When I Seek To Know Your Heart,
> I Will Find Such Blessed Assurance –
> In Your Holy Presence, Lord.

Some of the prerequisites for seeking the Lord and to be in His presence include - - -

1.   Being A Person of PRAYER

I THESSALONIANS 5:16-19
Be joyful always; pray continually; give thanks in all circums-tances, for this is God's will for you in Christ Jesus. Do not put out the Spirit's fire…

2.   Being A Person of FAITH

JAMES 2:18-26
But someone will say, You have faith; I have deeds. Show me your faith without deeds, and I will show you my faith by what I do. You believe that there is one God. Good! Even the demons believe that—and shudder. You foolish man, do you want evidence that faith without deeds is useless? Was not our ancestor Abraham considered righteous for what he did when he offered his son Isaac on the altar? You see that his faith and his actions were working together, and his faith was made complete by what he did. And the scripture was fulfilled that says, "Abraham believed God, and it was credited to him as righteousness," and he was called God's friend...As the body without the spirit is dead, so faith without deeds is dead.

3.   Being A Person Who Desires GOD'S WILL

COLOSSIANS 4:12
Epaphras...He is always wrestling in prayer for you, that you may stand firm in all the will of God, mature and fully assured.

JEREMIAH 29:11-14(a)
For I know the plans I have for you," declares the LORD, "plans to prosper you and not to harm you, plans to give you hope and a future. Then you will call upon me and come and pray to me, and I will listen to you. You will seek me and find me when you seek me with all your heart. I will be found by you," declares the LORD...

4.   Being A Person Who Seeks GOD'S GUIDANCE

PROVERBS 3:5-6

Trust in the LORD with all your heart and lean not on your own understanding; in all your ways acknowledge him, and he will make direct your paths (your paths straight).

A great truth to remember is - - -

ACTS 17:24-28
The God who made the world and everything in it is the Lord of heaven and earth and does not live in temples built by hands. And he is not served by human hands, as if he needed anything, because he himself gives all men life and breath and everything else. From one man he made every nation of men, that they should inhabit the whole earth; and he determined the times set for them and the exact places where they should live. God did this so that men would seek him and perhaps reach out for him and find him, though he is not far from each one of us. For in him we live and move and have our being.

A composition known As Saint Patrick's Breastplate is a Hymn – a portion of which includes one having the sense of being in God's presence always.

I bind unto myself today
The power of God to hold and lead,
His eye to watch, His might to stay,
His ear to hearken to my need.
The wisdom of my God to teach,
His hand to guide, His shield to ward;
The word of God to give me speech,
His heavenly host to be my guard.

Against the demon snares of sin,
The vice that gives temptation force,
The natural lusts that war within,
The hostile men that mar my course;

Or few or many, far or nigh,
In every place and in all hours,
Against their fierce hostility
I bind to me these holy powers.

Against all Satan's spells and wiles,
Against false words of heresy,
Against the knowledge that defiles,
Against the heart's idolatry,
Against the wizard's evil craft,
Against the death wound and the burning,
The choking wave, the poisoned shaft,
Protect me, Christ, till Thy returning.

Christ be with me, Christ within me,
Christ behind me, Christ before me,
Christ beside me, Christ to win me,
Christ to comfort and restore me.
Christ beneath me, Christ above me,
Christ in quiet, Christ in danger,
Christ in hearts of all that love me,
Christ in mouth of friend and stranger.

I bind unto myself the Name,
The strong Name of the Trinity,
By invocation of the same,
The Three in One and One in Three.
By Whom all nature hath creation,
Eternal Father, Spirit, Word:
Praise to the Lord of my salvation,
Salvation is of Christ the Lord.

May our purpose to walk with greater awareness and intimacy as
we learn what it means to walk and live in the presence of God.
May our prayer and desire always be - -

> Christ be with me, Christ within me,
> Christ behind me, Christ before me,
> Christ beside me, Christ to win me,
> Christ to comfort and restore me,
> Christ beneath me, Christ above me,
> Christ in quiet, Christ in danger,
> Christ in hearts of all that love me,
> Christ in mouth of friend and stranger....

Personal Study Questions - - -

How often are you totally aware that you are in God's presence?

Does it make a difference in what you say or do?

Does walking and living in the presence of God require any personal change in ones life? What would some be?

Can living in the presence of God be "taught" – or – is it most likely to be "caught"?

Do the words of Jesus in Matthew 11:20, "Take my yoke upon you and learn of Me?" have significant relevance? Who alone can be one's teacher in terms of what is meant by living in the presence of God?

Does the paraphrase of Matthew 11:29-30 in the New Living Translation help or confuse?

It states:

- "Take my yoke upon you. Let me teach you, because I am humble and gentle, and you will find rest for your souls. For my yoke fits perfectly, and the burden I give you is light."

Teaching Moments: God is an Ever-Present Help

Habakkuk 1:12-13

"Are you not from everlasting, O Lord my God, my Holy One?...You who are of purer eyes than to see evil and cannot look at wrong..."

Habakkuk is in a dialogue with God as he seeks to understand how a holy and just God can allow impurity and injustice to prevail within the culture of his day. The New Living Translation seems to capture the essence of Habakkuk's concerns in Habakkuk 1:12-17 (Selected) - O Lord my God, my Holy One, you who are eternal -- is your plan in all of this to wipe us out? Surely not! O Lord, our Rock, you have decreed the rise of these Babylonians to punish and correct us for our terrible sins. You are perfectly just in this. But will you, who cannot allow sin in any form, stand idly by while they swallow us up? Should you be silent while the wicked destroy people who are more righteous than they?...Will you let them get away with this forever? Will they succeed forever in their heartless conquests?" You may have formed similar questions as you've observed aberrant behavior within our culture seemingly go unchecked and uncontrolled. Aberrant Behavior – "departing from the right, normal, or usual course" - and - Abhorrent Behavior – "detestable; loathsome; utterly opposed, or contrary, or in conflict" – are sometimes linked by those who seek to cope with the evils of the day. It can lead to a question you may have posed and asked – "If there is a God Who cares and controls, why does He allow perverseness to prevail and righteousness to be rejected?" Or, "how long will He tolerated evil before He sends His judgment upon the earth?"

In a previous Chapter, there was a brief discussion on the non-communicable attributes of God – His Eternity, Omniscience, Omnipotence, Omnipresence and Immutability. In addition to these are the moral or communicable attributes of God that address and include: Goodness, Love, Mercy, Grace, Patience, Holiness, Peace, Righteousness (or Justice), Jealousy and Wrath. In this chapter, we'll consider two of the attributes in particular, namely jealousy and holiness.

From the Law of God, the attribute of the jealousy of God is stated forthrightly – Exodus 20:3-6, "You shall have no other gods before me. you shall not make for yourself a carved image, or any likeness of anything that is in heaven above, or that is in the earth beneath, or that is in the water under the earth. You shall not bow down to them or serve them, for I the Lord your God am a jealous God, visiting the iniquity of the fathers on the children to the third and the fourth generation of those who hate me, but showing steadfast love to thousands of those who love me and keep my commandments." The thought behind God saying that He is "jealous" pertains to when something that belongs to Him is given to another. In the Law, God is addressing people who make idols and bow down to worship the idols instead of bowing down to Him and giving Him the Glory, Honor and Praise that is due Him and His name alone.. God is possessive of the worship and service that belong to Him. It is a sin to worship or serve anything other than God. The force of this truth is emphatically underscored in Exodus 34:14, "…you shall worship no other god, for the Lord, whose name is Jealous, is a jealous God,"

The second attribute we'll consider is Holiness. We learn from Psalm 24:3, from a question that is posed: "Who shall ascend the hill of the LORD? And who shall stand in his holy place?" that the place God inhabits is a Holy Place. This is also reiterated in Psalm 99:9, "Exalt the Lord our God, and worship at his holy mountain; for the Lord our God is holy!" If one hopes to advance forward in living in the presence of God, then Holiness must be an increasing quality and reality in the life of the believer. Just a few verses to consider in this regard: Leviticus 19:2, "Speak to all the congregation of the people of Israel and say to them, You shall be holy, for I the Lord your God am holy." Additionally, we have the teaching of Hebrews 12:14 that stresses the importance and unequivocal necessity for the presence of Holiness within us if our focus on and commitment to God's Holiness is ones priority - "Strive for peace with everyone, and for the holiness without which no one will see the Lord." The rationale for how one is to pursue and attain Holiness is given in II Corinthians 7:1, "…let us cleanse ourselves from every defilement of body and spirit, bringing holiness to completion in the fear of God." Nothing less than this is God's requirement for walking and living in His presence.

When we contemplate the possibilities of living every moment of every day in the presence of God, we begin to learn the vastness and greatness of His being our ever-present help for all things at all times. As we consider the "every moment" in terms of the ever-present help of God, it's helpful to consider what a "moment" is (especially since we note in II Peter 3:8, "But do not overlook this one fact, beloved, that with the Lord one day is as a thousand years, and a thousand years as one day. It is obvious that the concept of "time" with God is neither confined nor restricted to the interpretation of time by mankind.)! American Heritage Dictionary Defines "Moment" as:

- A brief, indefinite interval of time.
- A specific point in time, especially the present time.
- A particular period of importance, influence.
- A brief period of time that is characterized by a quality, such as excellence, suitability, or distinction.

It is equally important to ask: "How do you define moments in and for your life? Is it an event or special occurrence – and then – detachment (or disconnect) until the next "moment" arrives? Or – Are your "moments" on a continuum – connected to all other moments in and for your life? An illustration of how God defines a moment is in I Corinthians 15:51-52, "Behold! I tell you a mystery. We shall not all sleep, but we shall all be changed,

- in a moment,
- in the twinkling of an eye,
- at the last trumpet.

For the trumpet will sound, and the dead will be raised imperishable, and we shall be changed." In God's mind, His "moment" is instantaneous in what He chooses to do and when He chooses to actuate it.

As we continue our pilgrimage with the Lord and learning more and more the possibilities and potential of walking and living every moment in the presence of God, we will also begin to learn that God is multi-dimensional. There are other attributes and truths concerning God - His decrees which are "...His eternal purpose, according to the counsel of his will, whereby, for his own glory, he hath foreordained whatsoever comes to pass." There is the knowledge of God and His foreknowledge; His Sovereignty; His Faithfulness, Goodness, Patience and Grace. The point is that one needs to think of and about God in the totality of Who He is and how He is with us always – every moment – all the time.

Acts 17:24-28(a) discusses the boundaries God established and why He had done so – "...God did this so that men would seek him and perhaps reach out for him and find him, though he is not far from each one of us. For in him we live and move and have our being..." In a similar way, the words in Deuteronomy 30:11-

16 reminds us – "…But the word is very near you. It is in your mouth and in your heart, so that you can do it. See, I have set before you today life and good, death and evil. If you obey the commandments of the Lord your God that I command you today, by loving the Lord your God, by walking in his ways, and by keeping his commandments and his statutes and his rules, then you shall live and multiply, and the Lord your God will bless you in the land that you are entering to take possession of it."

In religious literature , there is an interesting entry regarding the life and times of Brother Lawrence. "Brother Lawrence (1614-1691): began life as Nicholas Herman, born to peasant parents in Lorraine, France. As a young man, his poverty forced him into joining the army, and thus he was guaranteed meals and a small stipend.

"During this period, Herman had an experience that set him on a unique spiritual journey; it wasn't, characteristically, a super-natural vision, but a supernatural clarity into a common sight. In the deep of winter, Herman looked at a barren tree, stripped of leaves and fruit, waiting silently and patiently for the sure hope of summer abundance. Gazing at the tree, Herman grasped for the first time the extravagance of God's grace and the unfailing sovereignty of divine providence. Like the tree, he himself was seemingly dead, but God had life waiting for him, and the turn of seasons would bring fullness.

"An injury forced his retirement from the army, and after a stint as a footman, he sought a place where he could suffer for his failures. He thus entered the Discalced Carmelite Monastery in Paris as Brother Lawrence. He was assigned to the monastery kitchen where, amidst the tedious chores of cooking and cleaning at the constant bidding of his superiors, he developed his rule of spirituality and work. In his Maxims, Lawrence writes, - - -

"Men invent means and methods of coming at God's love, they learn rules and set up devices to remind them of that love, and it seems like a world of trouble to bring oneself into the consciousness of God's presence. Yet it might be so simple. Is it not quicker and easier just to do our common business wholly for the love of him?"

"Despite his somewhat lowly position, his character attracted many to him. He was known for his profound peace and many came to seek spiritual guidance from him. The wisdom that he passed on to them, in conversations and in letters, would later become the basis for the book, The Practice of the Presence of God." Brother Lawrence Stated Succinctly His Conviction and Motivation for One's Life - - -

"In the practice of the presence of God, we call Our Father to mind at every possible moment. At every opportunity, we focus our attention on Him and silently say, 'Thank You, Father' throughout each day.

"We should feed and nourish our soul with high notions of God which yield us great joy in being devoted to Him."

As we consider, every moment in the presence of our Ever-Present help, practical lessons can be gleaned from Exodus 23:20-32. The children of Israel are being prepared for The Conquest of Canaan. They will be reminded often that every moment they are In the presence of God – the Ever-Present Help. Within this preparation and instruction reminder, there is an encouragement to move forward and to persevere because God is preparing the way for them. Note some of these very practical words - - -

In Verse 20: An angel sent – To Guard them all along the way so they will be brought safely to the place He has prepared for them. It should remind one of the teaching of Jesus Christ in John 14:3

when He spoke with the uncertain and slightly disheartened Disciples, "If I go and prepare a place for you, I will come again and will take you to myself, that where I am you may be also." Jesus is asserting that H will bring us safely to the prepared place in our Canaan – Heaven.

In verses 21-22, the instruction is to pay careful attention to him. The angel who is guarding is the angel who will bring you safely to your destination. Therefore, you are to obey his voice and you are not to rebel against him. If that behavior is heeded and done, then there is the assurance in verse 23, "But if you carefully obey his voice and do all that I say, then I will be an enemy to your enemies and an adversary to your adversaries."

It is abundantly clear, based upon verses 24-25, that there can be no spiritual compromise. As the children of Israel approach Canaan, the directive is clear, namely, "you shall not bow down to their gods nor serve them." Don't get caught up or involved in what they have done or in what they are still doing. The commitment required by the Lord is, "...you shall utterly overthrow them and break their pillars in pieces...you shall serve the Lord your God." If these things are done, and continue to be done, the Lord states and assures: "I will bless your bread and your water, and I will take sickness away from among you." However, verses 32-33 state the place and need for added

Guardedness – "You shall make no covenant with them and their gods..." This is stating there will need to be a firm and continuing commitment to the posture of - no entangling alliances; no compromises; no accommodations. God is asserting that He says what He means and means what He says. A further requirement is: "They shall not dwell in your land, lest they make you sin against me; for if you serve their gods, it will surely be a snare to you." God is saying – 'Don't get cozy or comfortable with those who embrace false gods; have no unequal yoke with unbelievers.'

A reason for this instruction, guidance and mandate is given in Ephesians 5:10-12,. We are to "Try to discern what is pleasing to the Lord. Take no part in the unfruitful works of darkness, but instead expose them. For it is shameful even to speak of the things that they do in secret." The Message Paraphrase states: "Figure out what will please Christ, and then do it. Don't waste your time on useless work, mere busywork, the barren pursuits of darkness. Expose these things for the sham they are. It's a scandal when people waste their lives on things they must do in the darkness where no one will see."

As Martin Luther embarked on what became the reformation of the church – a truth that sustained him was Psalm 46:1-7, " God is our refuge and strength, an ever-present help in trouble. Therefore we will not fear, though the earth give way and the mountains fall into the heart of the sea, though its waters roar and foam and the mountains quake with their surging. There is a river whose streams make glad the city of God, the holy place where the Most High dwells. God is within her, she will not fall; God will help her at break of day. Nations are in uproar, kingdoms fall; he lifts his voice, the earth melts. The Lord Almighty is with us; the God of Jacob is our fortress." This same truth will sustain you every moment of every day – right here – right now…

With Psalm 46 firmly in his mind, Martin Luther would later write the words to a Hymn - - -

A mighty fortress is our God, a bulwark never failing;
Our helper He, amid the flood of mortal ills prevailing:
For still our ancient foe doth seek to work us woe;
His craft and power are great, and, armed with cruel hate,
On earth is not his equal.

And though this world, with devils filled,
should threaten to undo us,

We will not fear, for God hath willed
His truth to triumph through us:
The Prince of Darkness grim, we tremble not for him;
His rage we can endure, for lo, his doom is sure,
One little word shall fell him.

To begin to live every moment of every day in the presence of God, requires a restructuring of one's life and lifestyle - deliberately making oneself aware of God's Presence – every moment of every day. An old Bible Camp Song captures these thoughts and reassurances - - -

Every Moment of the Day – My Father Cares For Me!
Every Moment of the Day – My Heart From Fear Is Free!
He Who Sees The Sparrow Fall – Will Hear My Call –
Every Moment of the Day – God Watches Over Me!

Personal Study Questions - - -

Are you willing to make a commitment to live moment by moment in the presence of God…? Will You Try?

Are you willing to implement Ephesians 5:10-12 and have "…no part in the unfruitful works of darkness…"

To the best of your ability and commitment, are you ready and willing to reprove the unfruitful works of darkness? How, Where and When will you do this?

Always keep Psalm 46 in the forefront of your mind every moment of every day – "God is MY ever-present help…"

Always remind yourself – "I know that He never fails – and – He will never fail me." At any time or in any kind of trouble, you can depend upon Him. He is always available and always functional for every moment of every day for you. May your moments and days always know the reality of God's Presence.

Purposing to be in the Secret of His Presence

In 1887, Ellen L. Goreh was a high-caste native of India. After her conversion to Christianity, she spent some years in the home of an English clergyman, and wrote the poem that George C. Stebbins put to music – a Hymn that found almost immediate acceptance. The Cyber Hymnal has a history of the Hymn: "The hymn was first sung by George C. Stebbins as an offertory… It was often repeated as an offertory, and on occasions was sung in evangelistic services. But it had its larger introduction to the public during the All-Winter Mission conducted by Mr. Dwight L. Moody and Ira Sankey in London in the winter of 1883-84…Dr. Hudson Taylor, head of the great China Inland Mission, stated at Northfield [Massachusetts] that it was the favorite hymn of his missionaries…The words are - - -

In the secret of His presence how my soul delights to hide!
Oh, how precious are the lessons which I learn at Jesus' side!
Earthly cares can never vex me, neither trials lay me low;
For when Satan comes to tempt me, to the secret place I go,
To the secret place I go.

When my soul is faint and thirsty,
'neath the shadow of His wing
There is cool and pleasant shelter,
and a fresh and crystal spring;
And my Savior rests beside me, as we hold communion sweet:
If I tried, I could not utter what He says when thus we meet,
What He says when thus we meet.

Only this I know: I tell Him all my doubts, my griefs and fears;

Oh, how patiently He listens! And my drooping soul He
cheers:
Do you think He ne'er reproves me?
What a false Friend He would be,
If He never, never told me of the sins which He must see,
Of the sins which He must see.

It requires personal perseverance to find the path that leads one into being in the secret of His presence. When Jesus taught about which way to choose and how to find the right way, He said in Matthew 7:13-14 (ESV), "Enter by the narrow gate. For the gate is wide and the way is easy that leads to destruction, and those who enter by it are many. For the gate is narrow and the way is hard that leads to life, and those who find it are few." The Message Paraphrase states it in very basic language: "Don't look for shortcuts to God. The market is flooded with surefire, easygoing formulas for a successful life that can be practiced in your spare time. Don't fall for that stuff, even though crowds of people do. The way to life - to God! - is vigorous and requires total attention." This causes one to recall some of the lines from a Robert Frost poem about, The Road Less Traveled. Some of the lines from the poem are:

Two roads diverged in a yellow wood,
And sorry I could not travel both
And be one traveler, long I stood
And looked down one as far as I could
To where it bent in the undergrowth;

Then took the other, as just as fair,
And having perhaps the better claim,
Because it was grassy and wanted wear;
Though as for that the passing there
Had worn them really about the same,

And both that morning equally lay
In leaves no step had trodden black.
Oh, I kept the first for another day!
Yet knowing how way leads on to way,
I doubted if I should ever come back.

I shall be telling this with a sigh
Somewhere ages and ages hence:
Two roads diverged in a wood, and I--
I took the one less traveled by,
And that has made all the difference.

In some ways, the poem is humanistic and, if intended as a theological statement, could also be characterized as being more existential than not. The Existentialist is vague regarding what one will discover or uncover in the abyss of darkness but one should leap anyway, and in that leap, discover a faith that has found something out there. The point made by the Humanist and the Existentialist is that one should move in as positive a direction as possible, even though one has no solid determination of what awaits in and for the future. The Liberation Theology devotees feel they can put some "meat on the bones" as they approach a destiny with a philosophical persuasion that "...returns to the gospel of the early church where Christianity is politically and culturally decentralized... Liberation theology proposes to fight poverty by addressing its supposed source: sin. In so doing, it explores the relationship between Christian Theology – especially Roman Catholic Theology – and political activism, especially in terms of social justice, poverty, and human rights. Gustavo Gutierrez gave the movement its paradigmatic expression with his book A Theology of Liberation (1972). Gutierrez combined populist ideas with the social teachings of the Catholic Church... The book is based on an understanding of history in which the human being is seen as assuming conscious responsibility for human destiny, and yet Christ the Savior liberates the human race from sin, which is the root of all disruption of friendship and of all injustice and oppression..."

To indicate there is a world marked by theological confusion, is an understatement. Many of those expressing variant views are sincere and devoted to their persuasion and cause, however in all too many instances, they have missed the point of the message of Jesus Christ – and fall short, - because they are proven to be sincerely wrong in most of their conclusions.

Many times, the lessons one needs to learn are not easily and readily learned. There is an example of one who knew the tremendous power of God displayed in his behalf and through his ministry. As a matter of fact, after one of the more awesome displays of God's power through His servant, we find the prophet of God fearful and repairing to human frailty rather than abiding in the secret place of God's presence and the power that is found only there. We read about this event and experience in I Kings 19:1-13,

The Threat:
"Ahab told Jezebel all that Elijah had done, and how he had killed all the prophets with the sword. Then Jezebel sent a messenger to Elijah, saying, So may the gods do to me and more also, if I do not make your life as the life of one of them by this time tomorrow."

- Jezebel was more than annoyed with what Elijah had done. She spewed out her venomous invectives and aimed them directly at Elijah.
- There was no doubt about her intent. She wanted him dead and gone.

The Reaction:

"Then he (Elijah) was afraid, and he arose and ran for his life and came to Beersheba, which belongs to Judah, and left his servant there. But he himself went a day's journey into the wilderness and came and sat down under a broom tree. And he asked that he might die, saying: It is enough; now, O Lord, take away my life, for I am no better than my fathers. And he lay down and slept under a broom tree."

- Elijah had just dealt with the issue of the Prophets of Baal on Mount Carmel, and was very successful for the Lord there.
- Jezebel, the Queen, was displeased at what had occurred to the religious culture and practice in the land.
- She issues a death pronouncement that Elijah will be just like the false prophets, namely, death.
- Elijah's reaction – Flee in fear from the presence of the enemy - Jezebel!

God's Action:

"And behold, an angel touched him and said to him, Arise and eat. And he looked, and behold, there was at his head a cake baked on hot stones and a jar of water. And he ate and drank and lay down again. And the angel of the Lord came again a second time and touched him and said, Arise and eat, for the journey is too great for you. And he arose and ate and drank, and went in the strength of that food forty days and forty nights to Horeb, the Mount of God."

- Elijah allowed himself to forget all about the awesome power of God and His presence on Mount Carmel.
- The Angel's approach may actually have startled Elijah inasmuch as he had come to think that he was the last

Prophet of God left and now he was under a death sentence.

Prophet's Pity Party Moment:

"There he came to a cave and lodged in it. And behold, the word of the Lord came to him, and he said to him: What are you doing here, Elijah? He said: I have been very jealous for the Lord, the God of hosts. For the people of Israel have forsaken your covenant, thrown down your altars, and killed your prophets with the sword, and I, even I only, am left, and they seek my life, to take it away."

- Because of his conclusion based upon incorrect thinking and data, he was ready to die and be done with both the ministry opportunities and the Prophet for the Lord journey.

God's Getting His Prophet Back On Track:

And he said: Go out and stand on the mount before the Lord.

- And behold, the Lord passed by, and a great and strong wind tore the mountains and broke in pieces the rocks before the Lord, but the Lord was not in the wind.
- And after the wind an earthquake, but the Lord was not in the earthquake.
- And after the earthquake a fire, but the Lord was not in the fire.
- And after the fire the sound of a low whisper. And when Elijah heard it, he wrapped his face in his cloak and went out and stood at the entrance of the cave. And behold, there came a voice to him and said: What are you doing here, Elijah?

Obvious questions are: How does one anticipate and discern when he/she is in the presence of God? How do we expect Him to approach us? What method or means do we suppose He will employ to reach through all of one's confusion and fear to assure us that God is still there and remains in control? Being attentive and possessing an eager anticipation of Who God is and that He desires to commune and communicate with you is tantamount to knowing you have entered into the secret place of His Presence. Previously, we have noted the need for Living and Walking In The Presence of God. We Reflected On: Psalm 139:7-12,

"Where can I go from your Spirit? Where can I flee from your presence? If I go up to the heavens, you are there; if I make my bed in the depths, you are there. If I rise on the wings of the dawn, if I settle on the far side of the sea, even there your hand will guide me, your right hand will hold me fast."

We have observed that God and His Word is always very near. We saw this in Acts 17:24-28(a), "God did this so that men would seek him and perhaps reach out for him and find him, though he is not far from each one of us. For in him we live and move and have our being…" The idea is to keep on seeking the Lord while He can be found. This was also expounded in Deuteronomy 30:11-16, But the word is very near you. It is in your mouth and in your heart, so that you can do it. See, I have set before you today life and good, death and evil.

- Idea: Clear Choices Are Afforded One
- Life and Good – Death and Evil
- A Choice Must Be Made –
- Like Joshua: Choose Today Who/What You Will Serve!

We have noted that when Brother Lawrence was no longer able to cook meals, he was given the task of repairing and making sandals. He did that task with joy and peace because he did it for the glory of God. In his life, he sought to implement Colossians 3:12-17. He was always aware of the need and opportunity to practice the presence of God. The words of the text that impacted his life were, "Put on, as God's chosen ones, holy and beloved, compassionate hearts, kindness, humility, meekness, and patience, bearing with one another and, if one has a complaint against another, forgiving each other; as the Lord has forgiven you, so you also must forgive. And above all these put on love, which binds everything together in perfect harmony.

"And let the peace of Christ rule in your hearts, to which indeed you were called in one body. And be thankful.

"Let the word of Christ dwell in you richly, teaching and admonishing one another in all wisdom, singing psalms and hymns and spiritual songs, with thankfulness in your hearts to God.

"And whatever you do, in word or deed, do everything in the name of the Lord Jesus, giving thanks to God the Father through him."

Concern:

- our lives encounter many distractions - - -
- our focus becomes diverted - - -
- our commitments are too easily glossed over - - -
- we allow for too much clutter and contradiction - - -
- we allow our priorities and principles to be take a lesser place in our lives - - -

Sometimes our lives can encounter unexpected and unwanted obstacles, They can almost throw one off course and delay the ongoing walk with the Lord. It becomes easy to embrace a rationale of what is wrong and allows that correct behavior is too extreme. It can cause one to wonder momentarily about being in the presence of God and whether or not that is important, achievable and/or attainable. What causes this absurd thinking? What happens that causes one to think he can ignore the core beliefs of Biblical values?

Paul wrestled with this – and – describes it in Romans 7:15-24, "For I do not understand my own actions. For I do not do what I want, but I do the very thing I hate. Now if I do what I do not want, I agree with the law, that it is good. So now it is no longer I who do it, but sin that dwells within me. For I know that nothing good dwells in me, that is, in my flesh. For I have the desire to do what is right, but not the ability to carry it out. For I do not do the good I want, but the evil I do not want is what I keep on doing. Now if I do what I do not want, it is no longer I who do it, but sin that dwells within me. So I find it to be a law that when I want to do right, evil lies close at hand. For I delight in the law of God, in my inner being, but I see in my members another law waging war against the law of my mind and making me captive to the law of sin that dwells in my members. Wretched man that I am! Who will deliver me from this body of death?"

The Message Translation is: "What I don't understand about myself is that I decide one way, but then I act another, doing things I absolutely despise. So if I can't be trusted to figure out what is best for myself and then do it, it becomes obvious that God's command is necessary. But I need something more! For if I know the law but still can't keep it, and if the power of sin within me keeps sabotaging my best intentions, I obviously need help! I realize that I don't have what it takes. I can will it, but I can't do it. I decide to do good, but I don't really do it; I decide not to do bad, but then I do it anyway.

"My decisions, such as they are, don't result in actions. Something has gone wrong deep within me and gets the better of me every time.

"It happens so regularly that it's predictable. The moment I decide to do good, sin is there to trip me up. I truly delight in God's commands, but it's pretty obvious that not all of me joins in that delight. Parts of me covertly rebel, and just when I least expect it, they take charge. I've tried everything and nothing helps. I'm at the end of my rope. Is there no one who can do anything for me? Isn't that the real question?"

- Paul – was Unwilling To Accept This Vacillation and Context for his Life - - -
- He Did Not Want to Sacrifice Living and Walking In The Presence of God - - -

Romans 7:25 is his Resolve, Commitment, Answer – "Who will deliver me from this body of death? Thanks be to God through Jesus Christ our Lord! So then, I myself serve the law of God with my mind, but with my flesh I serve the law of sin."

The Message Translation is: "Is there no one who can do anything for me? The answer, thank God, is that Jesus Christ can and does. He acted to set things right in this life of contradictions where I want to serve God with all my heart and mind, but am pulled by the influence of sin to do something totally different."

Someone Drew Up A List of The 7 Deadly Sins. They Include:

Pride; Envy; Gluttony; Lust; Anger; Greed; Sloth. To counter these negatives, there is a Biblical starting point. It has a focus upon constructive virtues for the believer's life. In Colossians 3:12 - - -

"Put on, as God's chosen ones, holy and beloved, compassionate hearts, kindness, humility, meekness, and patience, bearing with one another..."

Philippians 4:8
"Finally, brothers, whatever is true, whatever is noble, whatever is right, whatever is pure, whatever is lovely, whatever is admirable--if anything is excellent or praiseworthy--think about such things."

The Message Paraphrase:

"Summing it all up, friends, I'd say you'll do best by filling your minds and meditating on things true, noble, reputable, authentic, compelling, gracious - the best, not the worst; the beautiful, not the ugly; things to praise, not things to curse…"

Classical Greek philosophers considered the foremost virtues to be: Prudence, temperance, courage, and justice. Early Christian Church theologians adopted these virtues and considered them to be equally important to all people, whether they were Christian or not. The Church Theologians Added The Obvious virtues from I Corinthians 13:13 - - - Faith, hope, love.

Additionally, Seven Contrary Virtues were Attached: Humility, kindness, abstinence, chastity, patience, liberality, diligence They were called contrary because they were contrasted to The Seven Deadly Sins. The idea and intention is to protect one against temptation toward the Seven Deadly Sins:

- Humility against pride,
- Kindness against envy,
- Abstinence against gluttony,
- Chastity against lust,
- Patience against anger,
- Liberality against greed, and
- Diligence against sloth.

If we are to enter more fully into the secret place of the presence of God, we must consider and apply additional basic truths. As you practice the presence of God in and for your life, consider:

Psalm 37:4-8

- "Delight yourself in the Lord and he will give you the desires of your heart.
- "Commit your way to the Lord; trust in him and he will do this: He will make your righteousness shine like the dawn, the justice of your cause like the noonday sun.
- "Be still before the Lord and wait patiently for him; do not fret when men succeed in their ways, when they carry out their wicked schemes.
- "Refrain from anger and turn from wrath; do not fret--it leads only to evil."

From: The Message - - -

- Keep company with God, get in on the best.
- Open up before God, keep nothing back; he'll do whatever needs to be done:
- He'll validate your life in the clear light of day and stamp you with approval at high noon.
- Quiet down before God, be prayerful before him. Don't bother with those who climb the ladder, who elbow their way to the top.
- Bridle your anger, trash your wrath, cool your pipes - it only makes things worse.

The poem containing the following words should be a daily reminder of one's need to continually seek to be and remain In The Secret Of His Presence:

In the secret of His presence how my soul delights to hide!

Oh, how precious are the lessons which I learn at Jesus' side!
Earthly cares can never vex me, neither trials lay me low;
For when Satan comes to tempt me, to the secret place I go.
To The Secret Place I Go!

Personal Study Questions - - -

Do you believe you have discovered where the secret place of His presence is? When did that occur.

What steps have you taken to safeguard that you will remain In The Secret of His Presence?

What things cause you to neglect or forget the secret place of His presence? How do you deal with it when it occurs?

How painful is it, personally, when you feel indifferent or aloof, perhaps too busy – any or all preventing you from being in the secret place of his presence rendezvous? How do you correct these feelings or attitudes?

We need to desire and walk in the reality of His Presence daily and free from distraction.

- Difficult? Yes!
- Necessary? Yes!
- Easy? No!
- Beneficial? Absolutely!

Endeavor to be as faithful and diligent as possible as you move forward into and maintain the growing reality – the committed purpose - of being in the secret place of His presence.

Focus: My Situation or God's Solution

One must be attuned to the moments with and the whispers from the Holy God. In a world and culture that is so oriented to the bombastic happenings and media bloviating (to talk aimlessly and boastingly), one can caught up in circumstances, situations and events while missing definitive truths and the accompanying nuances. Amid that context of living, one should establish particular verities and worthy goals for life:

- To Encounter God – getting to know him more
- To Experience God – trusting him and seeing his work in us…for us…through us in a greater way
- To Always Walk In His Ways – more faithfully and diligently…
- Maintaining the sense of Being In His Presence
- Learning to practice the presence of God

The Bible speaks of heaven as a place where God is uniquely present… Hebrews 9:24 - - -

"For Christ did not enter a man-made sanctuary that was only a copy of the true one; He entered heaven itself, now to appear for us in God's presence…"

- Inasmuch as we are in Christ positionally, we are also in God's Presence in actuality.

Luke 17:1-6 [NIV]

Jesus said to his disciples: Things that cause people to sin are bound to come, but woe to that person through whom they come. It would be better for him to be thrown into the sea with a millstone tied around his neck than for him to cause one of these little ones to sin. So watch yourselves. If your brother sins, rebuke him, & if he repents, forgive him. If he sins against you seven times in a day, and seven times comes back to you and says, I repent, forgive him. The apostles said to the Lord, Increase our faith! He replied, if you have faith as small as a mustard seed, you can say to this mulberry tree, Be uprooted and planted in the sea, and it will obey you.

The Message Paraphrase states:

"He said to his disciples, Hard trials and temptations are bound to come, but too bad for whoever brings them on! Better to wear a millstone necklace and take a swim in the deep blue sea than give even one of these dear little ones a hard time! Be alert. If you see your friend going wrong, correct him. If he responds, forgive him. Even if it's personal against you and repeated seven times through the day, and seven times he says, I'm sorry, I won't do it again, forgive him. The apostles came up and said to the Master, Give us more faith. But the Master said, You don't need more faith. There is no more or less in faith. If you have a bare kernel of faith, say the size of a poppy seed, you could say to this sycamore tree, Go jump in the lake, and it would do it.

A Few Years Back (1-25.06), an article by Gordon MacDonald appeared in Leadership Journal. He shared about driving his car for more than 25,000 miles without changing the oil. "On a cold New England morning, the car would not start. When the mechanic checked the engine, it was bound with thick sludge – it needed to be cleaned out…"

Problem:

- The situation with the engine took time, miles and neglect to produce the problem. It did not "just happen" or occur overnight.
- The solution to the problem would involve time and cost
- The process of cleaning out the sludge is not easy or simple – it will require hours of painstaking effort and will involve considerable cost.

An Application:

- What was true of the car, can also occur with the child of God. It results from carelessness or matter-of-factness – the idea that there is plenty of time yet to take care of a "small matter"!
- However, sludge buildup can occur in one's Spiritual life when one least expects it and when it is most inconvenient.
- The looming question is: "Are we willing to go through the process to get the sludge out?"

Hebrews 12:1 (NLT) states it this way: "…let us strip off every weight that slows us down, especially the sin that so easily hinders our progress. And let us run with endurance the race that God has set before us. In other words, Prioritize maintenance and be sure to get rid of all the sludge! Why?

- Sludge will affect the way we walk, run and think.
- Sludge will slow us down in our progress of daily practicing the presence of God in our lives

Philippians 1:6 is a faith principle for application. Paul wrote: "I am sure of this, that he who began a good work in you will bring it to completion at the day of Jesus Christ." It is helpful to attach this verse with Philippians 2:12, "Therefore, my beloved, as you have always obeyed, so now, not only as in my presence but much more in my absence, work out your own salvation with fear and trembling, for it is God who works in you, both to will and to work for his good pleasure." What application should be made from these verses?

- I will believe God is doing His good work in me.
- I will believe God is doing His work through me.
- I believe that God wants His children to be conscientious in all matters of His work in and through us.
- I am believing that God will enable me to finish well. God, who has begun a good work in me, will complete it!

By way of further application, some reflections from an experience in Elijah's life will be constructive. In I Kings 18-19, the following insights from his life and how quickly they can occur:

- The rapid descent from courage, boldness, fearlessness in I Kings 18
- To the rapid erosion that resulted in fear, flight, failure and depression in I Kings 19

Depression can quickly become one's reality and nightmare. Sometimes, there is no explanation or reason for it – it just seems to occur. Some of the synonyms for depression amplify more about what is at the root of this condition.

- abasement, cheerlessness, dejection, desolation,
- downheartedness, desperation, despondency
- discouragement and loss of self-worth
- fearfulness, gloominess, heaviness of heart,
- hopelessness, unhappiness, worry

Questions:

- How does a person move so rapidly from victory to defeat?
- What causes a person take his eyes off of a great victory and to focus on defeat?
- Why does a person who has everything to live for decide he has nothing to live for?
- What motivates one to snatch defeat out of the jaws of victory?
- What does it take to make one want to quit?

Sludge becomes a factor when one takes his/her eyes off of the solution and fixes them on his/her situation.

- People react and respond differently to difficult times…
- The longer the duration of the difficult times – ensuing acts or actions can become more drastic and urgent
- When faith seems to fail, despair emerges and dominates.

Sludge will tempt and cause one to take desperate & unusual measures - the enemy is relentless.

Sludge can also cause one to surrender faith and turn to hopelessness and death.

In the process, discernment is usually sacrificed and the issue of the moment takes control. Good news will often be met with:

- Skepticism …. Rationalization …. Apprehension
- Doubt… Fear … Suspicion
- Sludge can cause one to become Defeated and Fearful.

Elijah will never know the joy of the Lord in and for his life until he re-focuses on the presence of God. He needs to remember:

- God's will and God's ways are always best and right
- God will never leave or forsake him
- He is safely sheltered in the Lord's hand

An Old Camp Song/Chorus Contains These Words:

Safe am I, Safe am I, In the hollow of His hand;
Sheltered o'er, sheltered o'er, With His love forever more
No ill can harm me, No foe alarm me,
For He keeps both day and night,
Safe am I, Safe am I, In the hollow of His hand.

The child of God can never know the blessings and provisions of God fully unless and until he allows himself to move forward in faith. When one is actively pursuing the practice of the presence of God, too often there is a drift toward theory, and then procrastination occurs. One begins to hesitate regarding the things of faith and rationalization is quick to infiltrate the mind and thinking. And, all the while, the Lord is observing and asking:

- Why is it you have so little faith?
- Why do you doubt (Me)?
- Why do you hesitate to walk and live – conscious of my presence – day by day – and – moment by moment?
- Why have you divorced faith from believing in your daily walk with God?
- Why have you begun to doubt that God, who has begun a good work in you, will complete it?

In Luke 17:1, Jesus said: "Temptations to sin are sure to come…" One must be ready to exercise great care in order to resist the temptation(s) as and when they come. The Lord's Prayer included that necessary aspect, namely, "…and lead us not into temptation but deliver us from evil.." This must always be remembered and must be frequently prayed.

In Luke 17:3, Jesus said: "Pay attention to yourselves!" Jesus issues the reminder that the Christian Walk is a process that must demonstrate progress. Part of that progress Is In the care and influence one has in inter-personal relationships. The application Is given in Galatians 6:1-3, "Brothers, if anyone is caught in any transgression, you who are spiritual should restore him in a spirit of gentleness. Keep watch on yourself, lest you too be tempted. Bear one another's burdens, and so fulfill the law of Christ. For if anyone thinks he is something, when he is nothing, he deceives himself.

In Luke 17:3, Jesus also said: If your brother sins, rebuke him, and if he repents, forgive him…" It involves a hands-on ministry of care, concern, forgiveness, restoration. It is a follow-through of what Jesus taught in Matthew 6:14-15, "For if you forgive others their trespasses, your heavenly Father will also forgive you, but if you do not forgive others their trespasses, neither will your Father forgive your trespasses."

In Luke 17:5-6, there is a response to this instruction and direction by Jesus. "The Apostles said to the Lord, 'Increase our faith!' And the Lord said, If you had faith like a grain of mustard seed, you could say to this mulberry tree, Be uprooted and planted in the sea, and it would obey you." The implication for The Apostles is obvious – Do you believe this and in this way? Throughout His ministry with His disciples, Jesus would emphasize their need for a growing faith. Consider His concern for His followers regarding their practical needs, and their freedom from anxiety, Jesus taught them in Luke 12:27-28, "Consider the lilies, how they grow: they neither toil nor spin, yet I tell you, even Solomon in all his glory was not arrayed like one of these. But if God so clothes the grass, which is alive in the field today, and tomorrow is thrown into the oven, how much more will he clothe you, O you of little faith!"

In Matthew 8:23-26, Jesus wanted His disciples to look past the temporary storms one encounters in life, and to look always to Him for their safety and deliverance. "And when he got into the boat, his disciples followed him. And behold, there arose a great storm on the sea, so that the boat was being swamped by the waves; but he was asleep. And they went and woke him, saying, Save us, Lord; we are perishing. And he said to them, Why are you afraid, O you of little faith? Then he rose and rebuked the winds and the sea, and there was a great calm."

An old Hymn that is no longer sung very often, embraces the lessons Jesus wanted His followers to learn and know. The words are:

Master, the tempest is raging! The billows are tossing high!
The sky is o'er-shadowed with blackness,
No shelter or help is nigh;
Carest Thou not that we perish? How canst Thou lie asleep,
When each moment so madly is threatening
A grave in the angry deep?

Master, with anguish of spirit I bow in my grief today;
The depths of my sad heart are troubled
Oh, waken and save, I pray!
Torrents of sin and of anguish Sweep o'er my sinking soul;
And I perish! I perish! dear Master
Oh, hasten, and take control.

Master, the terror is over, The elements sweetly rest;
Earth's sun in the calm lake is mirrored,
And heaven's within my breast;
Linger, O blessed Redeemer! Leave me alone no more;

And with joy I shall make the blest harbor,
And rest on the blissful shore.

The Refrain:

The winds and the waves shall obey Thy will,
Peace, be still!
Whether the wrath of the storm tossed sea,
Or demons or men, or whatever it be,
No waters can swallow the ship where lies,
The Master of ocean, and earth, and skies;
They all shall sweetly obey Thy will,
Peace, be still! Peace, be still!
They all shall sweetly obey Thy will,
Peace, peace, be still!

To live as Jesus requires, the only option is to pray:

- Lord! – increase our faith!
- Lord! - increase my faith!
- I want to be free from clinging to my situations and my solutions!
- I want to cling to You and have You as my only solution!

A Child's Prayer Chorus that was sung many years ago contains a simple and basic truth for all today - - -

Into my heart, into my heart!
Come into my heart Lord Jesus!
Come in today! Come in to stay!
Come into my heart Lord Jesus!
Come into my life and control me completely!

Personal Study Questions - - -

In the ebb and flow of your life, the things you talk about with family or others, do they focus on personal issues, problems and frustrations – or – on God and God alone and His solutions?

If Jesus evaluated your faith today, how would he characterize it? No faith? Little faith? Great faith? What would cause Him to characterize it in that way?

In difficult economic times, or when the pains of life seem overwhelming, where would your focus be and which question would you ask God - - -

Why are you treating me this way and allowing me to be without and with these special needs?

Or - - -

What lesson(s) do you want me to learn from this moment in time – this situation?

I believe Romans 8:28 and Jeremiah 29:11, how does this fit into your perfect plan for my life?

Will storms and difficult times occur within one's lifespan? More than likely, they will. Will the grace of God sustain and prove to be more than sufficient? Most certainly, it will!

The Chorus from the B.B. McKinney Hymn, Have Faith In God, is an apt summary for all who believe – for all who aspire to be living in His Presence - - -

> Have faith in God, He's on His throne,
> Have faith in God, He watches over His own;
> He cannot fail, He must prevail,
> Have faith in God, Have faith in God.

Aura from Living in His Presence

The Glory of God and the aura of it – (aura defined: that subtle pervasive quality or atmosphere seen as emanating from a person, place, or thing) - was a very real experience for the people of God throughout their exodus journey and history. There is a beautiful description of God's relationship with His people as He led them out of Egypt into the direction of The Promised Land. The Presence of God was obvious as several miracles were performed in order that Pharaoh would let His people go. The ten plagues that impacted Egypt is one part of those miracles. A second part has a twofold impact for the Children of Israel, (a) The Cloud that would lead them, along with The Pillar of Fire that not only provided light for them at night, but also served to protect them from their enemies; and (b) the way God provided for their nourishment and sustenance – Manna from heaven and water from The Rock.

There were two other statements and stipulations made before God's people left Egypt. One is in Exodus 10:25-26, prior to the Ninth Plague – Darkness where Moses stipulated, "But Moses said, You must also let us have sacrifices and burnt offerings, that we may sacrifice to the Lord our God. Our livestock also must go with us; not a hoof shall be left behind, for we must take of them to serve the Lord our God, and we do not know with what we must serve the Lord until we arrive there." The point made is "not a hoof shall be left behind." The other is in Exodus 11:2, 6-7: "Speak now in the hearing of the people, that they ask, every man of his neighbor and every woman of her neighbor, for silver and gold jewelry…There shall be a great cry throughout all the land of Egypt, such as there has never been, nor ever will be again. But not a dog shall growl against any of the people of Israel, either man or beast, that you may know that the Lord makes a distinction between Egypt and Israel." They will leave with riches and possessions given to them by the Egyptians, and when they leave – not a dog of the Egyptians will growl or bark. It should've proven to God's people that if He could control the growl and bark of a dog, He would protect them on their journey and silence all their enemies.

There is a special moment in the life of Moses as he gets alone with God for a time of intercession. A few excerpts of that special moment are taken from Exodus 33:12-23, "Moses said to the Lord...if I have found favor in your sight, please show me now your ways, that I may know you in order to find favor in your sight. Consider too that this nation is your people. And the Lord said, My presence will go with you, and I will give you rest. And Moses said to him, If your presence will not go with me, do not bring us up from here...And the Lord said to Moses, This very thing that you have spoken I will do, for you have found favor in my sight, and I know you by name. Moses said, Please show me your glory. And the Lord said, I will make all my goodness pass before you and will proclaim before you my name The Lord...But...you cannot see my face, for man shall not see me and live...Behold, there is a place by me where you shall stand on the rock, and while my glory passes by I will put you in a cleft of the rock, and I will cover you with my hand until I have passed by. Then I will take away my hand, and you shall see my back, but my face shall not be seen."

The aftermath of this intercession is given in Exodus 34:5-9, The Lord descended in the cloud and stood with him there, and proclaimed the name of the Lord...The Lord, the Lord, a God merciful and gracious, slow to anger, and abounding in steadfast love and faithfulness, keeping steadfast love for thousands, forgiving iniquity and transgression and sin, but who will by no means clear the guilty...And Moses quickly bowed his head toward the earth and worshiped…" When one spends time alone in the presence of the Lord, it will make a significant difference in one's life. Once one has been effectually called, justified, adopted in the family of God, and sanctified – there will be a difference – there must be a difference - in the way in which one walks and talks and lives from that point forward. A result of these moments Moses spent in intercession with The Lord is described in Exodus 34:29-35, "When Moses came down from Mount Sinai, with the two tablets of the testimony in his hand as he came down from the mountain, Moses did not know that the skin of his face shone because he had been talking with God. Aaron and all the people of Israel saw Moses, and behold, the skin of his face shone, and they were afraid to come near him…Afterward all the people of Israel came near, and he commanded them all that the Lord had spoken with him in Mount Sinai. And when Moses had finished speaking with them, he put a veil over his face. Whenever Moses went in before the Lord to speak with him, he would remove the veil, until he came out. And when he came out and told the people of Israel what he was commanded, the people of Israel would see the face of Moses, that the skin of Moses' face was shining. And Moses would put the veil over his face again, until he went in to speak with the Lord again." There should be – must be - a noticeable difference in one's appearance after spending time with The Lord.

When Peter and John were before the Council and told they were no longer to proclaim the Gospel, a glimpse of what occurred is shared in Acts 4:12-13 when Peter and John respond, "…there is salvation in no one else, for there is no other name under heaven given among men by which we must be saved. Now when they (the Council) saw the boldness of Peter and John, and perceived that they were uneducated, common men, they were astonished. And they recognized that they had been with Jesus." The Council could not escape the facts or come to any other conclusion than – "They recognized that they had been with Jesus." It was a conclusion that these were men who had been – and who were continuing to be – living in the Presence of God.

Living in the Presence of God was to be an ongoing experience and reality for the children of Israel. The Cloud that went before the people is often referred to as The Shekhinah Glory Cloud because it represented the presence of God with and for His people. A significant statement regarding this glory cloud is given in Exodus 40:34-38, "Then the cloud covered the tent of meeting, and the glory of the Lord filled the tabernacle. And Moses was not able to enter the tent of meeting because the cloud settled on it, and the glory of the Lord filled the tabernacle. Throughout all their journeys, whenever the cloud was taken up from over the tabernacle, the people of Israel would set out. But if the cloud was not taken up, then they did not set out till the day that it was taken up. For the cloud of the Lord was on the tabernacle by day, and fire was in it by night, in the sight of all the house of Israel throughout all their journeys.." What did this mean for the people of God and all their enemies? Simply and plainly - that God was in the midst of His people. The people of God needed to realize and reckon with all of what that meant; and the enemies of God's people needed to realize and reckon that if they sought to harm God's people, they would be sorely punished.

Years later, after Solomon has completed building the Temple in Jerusalem, I Kings 8:6-11 (Selected) records the following, "Then the priests brought the ark of the covenant of the Lord to its place in the inner sanctuary of the house, in the Most Holy Place…There was nothing in the ark except the two tablets of stone that Moses put there at Horeb, where the Lord made a covenant with the people of Israel, when they came out of the land of Egypt. And when the priests came out of the Holy Place, a cloud filled the house of the Lord, so that the priests could not stand to minister because of the cloud, for the glory of the Lord filled the house of the Lord." What was that cloud? It was the cloud that had been with them for forty years in the wilderness. It was the same cloud that led them on their journey and protected them from their enemies. It represented the continual glory and presence of God with His people.

There is a Worship Chorus that incorporates the idea of the presence of God in the midst of His people based upon the picture one has of the Cloud hovering over the Tabernacle and the Cloud entering the Holy of Holies in the Temple. The words, usually sung with feeling and emotion, are:

> Oh the glory of Your presence,
> We Your people give You reverence,
> So arise from Your rest
> and be blessed by our praise,
> As we glory in Your embrace
> and Your presence now fills this place.

The words express how it should be in the House of the Lord. The question is: "How many places and times has that been a valid description or demonstration of what is taking place when 'The Church' assembles for public worship of God?" Does the routine and ritual designed by man interrupt and interfere with any possibility of God being in the midst of His people today? In another Worship Chorus, designed to suggest and convince the gathered people of an experience they either will or have had a unique time when they assembled, states:

> There's a sweet, sweet Spirit in this place
> And I know that it's the Spirit of the Lord.
> There are sweet expressions on each face
> And I know they feel the presence of the Lord.
>
> Sweet Holy Spirit, sweet Heavenly Dove -
> Stay right here with us,

Filling us with Your love.
And for these blessings we lift our hearts in praise
Without a doubt we know that we'll have been revived
When we shall leave this place.

Just saying it or singing it doesn't make it a reality. The reality in worship comes from a heart that is in a correct relationship with the Lord Jesus Christ. How can and does one enter into true worship of God? When Jesus spoke and taught about true worship, He encapsulated in His interaction with The Samaritan Woman – the woman at the well – how one can properly and adequately worship God. In John 4:19-24, "The woman said to him, Sir, I perceive that you are a prophet. Our fathers worshiped on this mountain, but you say that in Jerusalem is the place where people ought to worship. Jesus said to her, Woman, believe me, the hour is coming when neither on this mountain nor in Jerusalem will you worship the Father. You worship what you do not know; we worship what we know, for salvation is from the Jews. But the hour is coming, and is now here, when the true worshipers will worship the Father in spirit and truth, for the Father is seeking such people to worship him. God is spirit, and those who worship him must worship in spirit and truth." What is the "true worship" Jesus is speaking about? He says:

- true worshipers will worship the Father in spirit and truth
- those who worship him must worship in spirit and truth

In any kind of an exhaustive study on the subject of "glory", one would find an almost endless supply of references on that word and subject. For this study, the handful for study include - -

John 1:14-16 – The Birth and Physical Presence of Jesus Christ

:And the Word became flesh and dwelt among us, and we have seen his glory, glory as of the only Son from the Father, full of grace and truth…And from his fullness we have all received, grace upon grace."

In terms of "we have seen His glory, glory as of the only Son from the Father", Matthew Henry comments:

"By his Divine presence Christ always was in the world. But now that the fullness of time was come, he was, after another manner, God manifested in the flesh. But observe the beams of his Divine glory, which darted through this veil of flesh. Men discover their weaknesses to those most familiar with them, but it was not so with Christ; those most intimate with him saw most of his glory. Although he was in the form of a servant, as to outward circumstances, yet, in respect of graces, his form was like the Son of God His Divine glory appeared in the holiness of his doctrine, and in his miracles. He was full of grace, fully acceptable to his Father, therefore qualified to plead for us; and full of truth, fully aware of the things he was to reveal."

Hebrews 1:1-4 expands on the John 1:14 reference and adds:

"Long ago, at many times and in many ways, God spoke to our fathers by the prophets, but in these last days he has spoken to us by his Son, whom he appointed the heir of all things, through whom also he created the world. He is the radiance of the glory of God and the exact imprint of his nature, and he upholds the universe by the word of his power. After making purification for sins, he sat down at the right hand of the Majesty on high, having become as much superior to angels as the name he has inherited is more excellent than theirs."

IN one sense, the full and complete Glory of God in the earthly life and ministry of the Lord Jesus Christ must include the action agreed upon by the Godhead when Jesus Christ was preparing to come to earth. Philippians 2:5-8 shares, "Have this mind among yourselves, which is yours in Christ Jesus, who, though he was in the form of God, did not count equality with God a thing to be grasped, but made himself nothing, taking the form of a servant, being born in the likeness of men. And being found in human form, he humbled himself by becoming obedient to the point of death, even death on a cross." These same verses from the New Living Translation share the idea that while Jesus was God, He was willing to set aside His prerogatives (an exclusive right, privilege, etc., exercised by virtue of rank, office) of His Glory when He agreed to come to earth. From the NLT, "Your attitude should be the same that Christ Jesus had. Though he was God, he did not demand and cling to his rights as God. He made himself nothing; he took the humble position of a slave and appeared in human form. And in human form he obediently humbled himself even further by dying a criminal's death on a cross." The focus is on the phrase in Hebrews 1: "He is the radiance of the glory of God and the exact imprint of his nature..." , Matthew Henry comments,

"When, on the fall of man, the world was breaking to pieces under the wrath and curse of God, the Son of God, undertaking the work of redemption, sustained it by his almighty power and goodness. From the glory of the person and office of Christ, we proceed to the glory of his grace. The glory of His person and nature, gave to his sufferings such merit as was a full satisfaction to the honor of God, who suffered an infinite injury and affront by the sins of men."

The Apostle Paul speaks to how the Glory of God enters and penetrates a believer's life. In II Corinthians 4:6-7, he writes:

"For God, who said, Let light shine out of darkness has shone in our hearts to give the light of the knowledge of the glory of God in the face of Jesus Christ. But we have this treasure in jars of clay, to show that the surpassing power belongs to God and not to us."

The focus phrase is: "For God…has shone in our hearts to give the light of the knowledge of the glory of God in the face of Jesus Christ. If our body is a temple, and if the Gospel has entered into the temple, and if Jesus Christ has become part of one's body, soul and spirit – wherever Jesus is present – His glory is also present. There needs to be evidence of this in a professing Christians walk, talk and life. Francis Schaeffer wrote about The Distinguishing Mark of the Christian:

"My children, I will be with you only a little longer. You will look for me, and just as I told the Jews, so I tell you now: Where I am going, you cannot come. A new command I give you: Love one another. As I have loved you, so you must love one another. By this all men will know that you are my disciples, if you love one another." (John 13:33-35) This passage reveals the mark that Jesus gives to label a Christian not just in one era or in one locality but at all times and all places until Jesus returns. Notice that what he says here is not a description of a fact. It is a command which includes a condition: "A new command I give you: Love one another. As I have loved you, so you must love one another. By this all men will know that you are my disciples, if you love one another." An if is involved. If you obey, you will wear the badge Christ gave. But since this is a command, it can be violated. The point is that it is possible to be a Christian without showing the mark, but if we expect non-Christians to know that we are Christians, we must show the mark."

Personal Study Questions - - -

When you're in a group of people, do they sense and know that you have been with Jesus? How? Why?

Is there a noticeable difference in your life – an aura about you - because of the times of intercession you have with The Lord? In your case, what is it?

When Paul wrote that "your attitude should be the same that Christ Jesus had", what do you think that means and includes?

If your attitude is the same that The Lord Jesus Christ had, how do you think people will respond to you? Will it usually be positive, or more than likely, negative? Why?

May the Lord fill you with His presence and cause you to be an effective Christian and an adequate representative for Him.

II Corinthians 5:20

"Therefore, we are ambassadors for Christ, God making his appeal through us. We implore you on behalf of Christ, be reconciled to God."

When God's Presence is Removed

Could it be that God's Presence could become a spoil of war? Did an enemy army decide that capturing The Ark would demoralize their opponent and result in their defeat? Was that conquest construed to mean that whatever benefit Israel had received from the presence of The Ark would now transfer to the Philistines?

The Day God's Glory Was Removed, or The Day God's Glory Departed would make a useful contribution to the world of literature and the Church after the manner of the tomes written by Jim Bishop. A Wikipedia entry states: An easy-to-read writer was James Alonzo "Jim" Bishop (1907-1987) who spent considerable years as a newspaper reporter. The remainder of his career, from 1955, was spent writing biographical books about notable figures, and Christian-themed books. His book The Day Lincoln Was Shot was published in 1955, and became an instant best-seller. Bishop also wrote The Day Christ Died, The Day Christ Was Born, and The Day Kennedy Was Shot. Perhaps his most critically acclaimed book was FDR's Last Year: April 1944-April 1945, which brought to public awareness the secrecy that surrounded President Franklin D. Roosevelt's declining health during World War II. It would've been fitting to include a title along these lines, such as, The Day The Glory Departed, and developing the cause-behaviors that resulted in that departure from the midst of His people.

There are Two Scriptural Scenarios to consider regarding the departure of God's Glory. The First Scenario is seen in the report of I Samuel 4:10-11. It would prove to be a very sad day in Israel and for Eli. Note the report:

"So the Philistines fought, and Israel was defeated, and they fled, every man to his home. And there was a very great slaughter, for there fell of Israel thirty thousand foot soldiers. And the ark of God was captured, and the two sons of Eli, Hophni and Phinehas, died."

It was a tragic day and a considerable defeat. There was (a) a great slaughter as thirty-thousand foot soldiers were killed, (b) The Ark of God was captured, and (c) the two sons of Eli the Priest were now dead. What else could happen? What further calamity would occur? The calamity continues as the report is delivered to Eli. This appears in I Samuel 4:17-21,

"He who brought the news to Eli answered and said Israel has fled before the Philistines, and there has also been a great defeat among the people; Your two sons also, Hophni and Phinehas, are dead and the ark of God has been captured. As soon as he mentioned the ark of God, Eli fell over backward from his seat by the side of the gate, and his neck was broken and he died...his daughter-in-law, the wife of Phinehas, was pregnant, about to give birth. And when she heard the news that the ark of God was captured, and that her father-in-law and her husband were dead, she bowed and gave birth, for her pains came upon her. And about the time of her death the women attending her said to her, Do not be afraid, for you have borne a son...And she named the child Ichabod, saying, The glory has departed from Israel! because the ark of God had been captured and because of her father-in-law and her husband. And she said, The glory has departed from Israel, for the ark of God has been captured."

The child born is given the name Ichabod meaning the Glory of God has departed from Israel. The Ark has been captured by a fierce and strong enemy. The troops of Israel have been decimated. They have no way of recovering The Ark. They are overwhelmed in their despair and hopelessness. The clear thought of the remaining people is:

- God is no longer with us!
- God is no longer in our midst!
- The Glory of God is no longer visibly present and physically present with us!
- We are helpless to go and retrieve it!

They had grown accustomed to having God in their midst. In a very strange way, they depended upon God continuing to be with them. It was like "good luck" for them! They did not think through what was occurring or why it was so severe. They did not reflect upon their ignoring of God's purpose and standard for them. They did not consider their own willfulness had become their lifestyle of choice. They should've asked and answered:

- Have we taken the Lord for granted? Yes!
- Have we ignored Him in worship? Yes!
- Have we disobeyed His precepts? Yes!

Interestingly, the Philistines would quickly come to regret their capture of The Ark of the Covenant. It brought them nothing but grief day-after-day. In I Samuel 5:1-12, after they brought The Ark to Ashdod, the unexpected took place.

 In verses 1-6, "When the Philistines captured the ark of God, they brought it from Ebenezer to Ashdod. Then the Philistines took the ark of God and brought it into the house of Dagon and set it up beside Dagon. And when the people of Ashdod rose early the next day, behold, Dagon had fallen face downward on the ground before the ark of the Lord. So they took Dagon and put him back in his place. But when they rose early on the next morning, behold, Dagon had fallen face downward on the ground before the ark of the Lord, and the head of Dagon and both his hands were lying cut off on the threshold. Only the trunk of Dagon was left to him...The hand of the Lord was heavy against the people of Ashdod, and he terrified and afflicted them with tumors, both Ashdod and its territory."

The Philistines may have disdained The God of Israel but now they have to begin to reckon with Him. Once they bring The Ark of God into their cities they soon discover there is a major consequence for mocking and disdaining God. It reminds one that God, the Lord is never left without a witness. He will always utilize various means to make His Name known among the nations. There is a definitive scene in Luke 19:37-40, "As he was drawing near, already on the way down the Mount of Olives, the whole multitude of his disciples began to rejoice and praise God with a loud voice for all the mighty works that they had seen, saying, Blessed is the King who comes in the name of the Lord! Peace in heaven and glory in the highest! And some of the Pharisees in the crowd said to him, Teacher, rebuke your disciples. He answered, I tell you, if these were silent, the very stones would cry out." It is not the Philistines as the enemy but the Pharisees who have stepped forward as the opposition. The Lord will never leave Himself without a witness. Either the very stones crying out, or a pagan god bowing down, or the trees of the field clapping their hands, or a donkey rebuking its rider – there will be recognition and worship of The Lord and a witness about Him. He will be heard and make His Presence known.

The Philistines have moved from exuberance about their victory over Israel to gloom and despair as serious and negative physical maladies are seemingly everywhere. Wherever they take The Ark, people become ill and distraught. In I Samuel 5:7-10, "And when the men of Ashdod saw how things were, they said, The ark of the God of Israel must not remain with us, for his hand is hard against us and against Dagon our god. So they sent and gathered together all the lords of the Philistines and said, What shall we do with the ark of the God of Israel? They answered, Let the ark of the God of Israel be brought around to Gath. So they brought the ark of the God of Israel there. But after they had brought it around, the hand of the Lord was against the city, causing a very great panic, and he afflicted the men of the city, both young and old, so that tumors broke out on them." They assessed their situation correctly, (a) the hand of God is hard against them and their god Dagon, and (b) all age groups were being afflicted with tumors.

It serves as a reminder that God is not mocked. God is to be honored and recognized for Who He is. There is always conse-quence for those who view God as something or someone other than Who He Is – the Eternal God, the Creator and Sustainer of all things. The people of Gath suffered greatly because The Ark was viewed as a trophy of war and was ignored as representing the presence of God and His glory. To alleviate their consequence for having The Ark, they arrive at a decision – pass it off to someone else. We find in I Samuel 5:10-12, "So they sent the ark of God to Ekron. But as soon as the ark of God came to Ekron, the people of Ekron cried out, They have brought around to us the ark of the God of Israel to kill us and our people. They sent therefore and gathered together all the lords of the Philistines and said, Send away the ark of the God of Israel, and let it return to its own place, that it may not kill us and our people. For there was a deathly panic throughout the whole city. The hand of God was very heavy there. The men who did not die were struck with tumors, and the cry of the city went up to heaven." Great suffer-ing and anguish became the experience of the people. The hand of God was very heavy upon them.

What should the Philistines do when God's hand is heavy upon them? What is the most reasonable action they can take? Shall they stubbornly resist God's hand as the Egyptians and Pharaoh did earlier? Should they convert, believe and be healed? What is the most reasonable alternative for them? They arrive at their decision and in I Samuel 6, after seven months of anguish, harm and hardship - they arrive at a conclusion. "The ark of the Lord was in the country of the Philistines seven months. And the Philistines called for the priests and the diviners and said, What shall we do with the ark of the Lord? Tell us with what we shall send it to its place…Now then, take and prepare a new cart and two milk cows on which there has never come a yoke, and yoke the cows to the cart, but take their calves home, away from them. And take the ark of the Lord and place it on the cart and put in a box at its side the figures of gold, which you are returning to him as a guilt offering. Then send it off and let it go its way and watch. If it goes up on the way to its own land, to Beth-shemesh, then it is he who has done us this great harm, but if not, then we shall know that it is not his hand that struck us; it happened to us by coincidence…And the cows went straight in the direction of Beth-shemesh along one highway, lowing as they went. They turned neither to the right nor to the left, and the lords of the Philistines went after them as far as the border of Beth-shemesh. Now the people of Beth-shemesh were reaping their wheat harvest in the valley. And when they lifted up their eyes and saw the ark, they rejoiced to see it…"

The Ark is returning to its place in the midst of the children of Israel. Will they respond any differently to the Presence of God in their midst now, or will they continue in their routines and matter-of-fact manner of living? They have a unique moment that allows them the opportunity to recommit themselves to The Lord and to seek His ways only. Will they have the good sense to do it? Will they begin to take God seriously? Will they read and heed God's Word? Just so they would no longer take Him for granted and carelessly approach Him, there is this incident noted in I Samuel 6:19-21, "And he struck some of the men of Beth-shemesh, because they looked upon the ark of the Lord. He struck seventy men of them, and the people mourned because the Lord had struck the people with a great blow. Then the men of Beth-shemesh said, Who is able to stand before the Lord, this holy God? And to whom shall he go up away from us? So they sent messengers to the inhabitants of Kiriath-jearim, saying, "The Philistines have returned the ark of the Lord. Come down and take it up to you." The Lord is establishing once again (a) don't trifle with the things of God, (b) don't be matter-of-fact regarding spiritual matters, (c) be serious and reverent about the Lord and all that pertains to Him, and (d) don't miss out on His Blessing for those who are obedient to Him.

Twenty years have now passed since The Ark had been returned to Israel. In I Samuel 7:2-8, the children of Israel come to Samuel and ask for his intercession with The Lord in their behalf. Twenty years before the people getting back on track in terms of their relationship to and with the Lord. The text states: "...all the house of Israel lamented after the Lord. And Samuel said to all the house of Israel, "If you are returning to the Lord with all your heart, then put away the foreign gods and the Ashtaroth from among you and direct your heart to the Lord and serve him only, and he will deliver you out of the hand of the Philistines. So the people of Israel put away the Baals and the Ashtaroth, and they served the Lord only. Then Samuel said, Gather all Israel at Mizpah, and I will pray to the Lord for you. So they gathered at Mizpah and drew water and poured it out before the Lord and fasted on that day and said there, We have sinned against the Lord. And Samuel judged the people of Israel at Mizpah. Now when the Philistines heard that the people of Israel had gathered at Mizpah, the lords of the Philistines went up against Israel. And when the people of Israel heard of it, they were afraid of the Philistines. And the people of Israel said to Samuel, Do not cease to cry out to the Lord our God for us, that he may save us from the hand of the Philistines." The Lord does save them from the hand of this persistent enemy. However, after this defeat at Mizpah, the Philistines will not soon return.

Just as an aside, it is interesting to note one of the meanings of the term Mizpah. The idea is one of a watch-tower of a place where there is a lookout. It is associated with Jacob and Laban. The Bible Dictionary states: "A place in Gilead, so named by Laban, who overtook Jacob at this spot (Genesis 31:49) on his return to Palestine from Padan-aram. Here Jacob and Laban set up their memorial cairn of stones." It carries a meaning of: "The Lord watch between me and you, while we are absent one from the other." With Jacob involved, it was also a matter of trust and integrity.

Several years have passed and Samuel has anointed Saul to be their king. He will also anoint the man after God's own heart – David – who will be God's king among the people. After David ascends to the throne, The Ark of God is going to be moved to Jerusalem. The narrative is in II Samuel 6-9. It begins with these words in I Samuel 6:1-15, "David again gathered all the chosen men of Israel, thirty thousand. And David arose and went with all the people who were with him…And they carried the ark of God on a new cart and brought it out of the house of Abinadab…And David and all the house of Israel were making merry before the Lord, with songs and lyres and harps and tambourines and castanets and cymbals…But David took it aside to the house of Obed-edom the Gittite. And the ark of the Lord remained in the house of Obed-edom the Gittite three months, and the Lord blessed Obed-edom and all his household. And it was told King David, "The Lord has blessed the household of Obed-edom and all that belongs to him, because of the ark of God. So David went and brought up the ark of God from the house of Obed-edom to the city of David with rejoicing. And when those who bore the ark of the Lord had gone six steps, he sacrificed an ox and a fattened animal. And David danced before the Lord with all his might…So David and all the house of Israel brought up the ark of the Lord with shouting and with the sound of the horn…" After years and months, The Ark is returned into the midst of the people once more. The people must focus upon God in their midst if they are to know Him and benefit from His blessings for them.

In the average Christian life, there are observable cycles. When one experiences new birth in Christ, there is wonderment and an eagerness to learn about Christ. In the next cycle, as one develops, there is a continued eagerness to serve and to present the Gospel of Jesus Christ to others. At a future point, the cycle reaches a plateau and a complacency enters where there once had been eagerness. Growth in the grace and knowledge of the Lord Jesus Christ has almost halted and rather than one being in gear and accelerating, neutrality has become the choice and one is coasting. In part, this is what occurred with the children of Israel and the Ark of God. The Ark was no longer the necessary center of daily life as it once had been. The Ark was there and the people wanted it in their midst – it's just that they were not as excited about it as they once had been. They were complacent, matter-of-fact and had become ambivalent. It can happen too quickly and to anyone. They needed to return to a constancy of seeking the Lord while He may be found and calling upon Him while He is still near.

Personal Study Questions - - -

Do you have the enthusiasm and eagerness that you had when you first turned to Jesus Christ as Savior? Briefly describe what that was like!

Is The Lord the center of your life and lifestyle? Is He preeminent (Colossians 1:18) in all things that pertain to you? Explain in what ways this would be true!

If you are complacent about some things, why do you believe that is the case? How did you arrive at that place in your life?

Is God's Presence a constant and continuing reality for you?

There is a meaningful Hymn of Consecration entitled All For Jesus. Is it the Hymn of your Heart?

> All for Jesus, all for Jesus!
> All my being's ransomed powers:
> All my thoughts and words and doings,
> All my days and all my hours.
>
> Let my hands perform His bidding,
> Let my feet run in His ways;
> Let my eyes see Jesus only,
> Let my lips speak forth His praise.
>
> Worldlings prize their gems of beauty,
> Cling to gilded toys of dust,
> Boast of wealth and fame and pleasure;
> Only Jesus will I trust.
>
> Since my eyes were fixed on Jesus,
> I've lost sight of all beside;
> So enchained my spirit's vision,
> Looking at the Crucified.
>
> Oh, what wonder! How amazing!
> Jesus, glorious King of kings,
> Deigns to call me His beloved,
> Lets me rest beneath His wings.

Make this the song of your heart and soul – the song of a heart set free by Jesus Christ – and that is now completely committed to Him.

The Return of the Glory of His Presence

What will it take for the glory of the Lord to return into the midst of the children of Israel? Will it remain with them? What will it take for the Glory of God to return into the midst of His people today? What will be required of "The Church" before it can and will happen? Is it a realistic expectation to contemplate the return of the Glory of His Presence? There are many efforts and movements attempting to restore, renew and revitalize "The Church" to its more complete function. Are they succeeding? Will they succeed?

After The Ark is retrieved and returns to the City of David, heading toward its destination in Jerusalem, there are important steps that must be taken. David will have to serve out his reign as King but he will not be permitted to build a permanent Temple that will house The Ark and the Presence of God in the center of the nation. He will have to come to an understanding of God's will and purpose and be reconciled to it. Will it be easy for him to hear God's plan and to comply with it? The explanation of God's purpose and plan is given in II Samuel 7:1-17 (Selected), "Now when the king lived in his house and the Lord had given him rest from all his surrounding enemies, the king said to Nathan the prophet, See now, I dwell in a house of cedar, but the ark of God dwells in a tent…that same night the word of the Lord came to Nathan, Go and tell my servant David…Thus says the Lord of hosts, I took you from the pasture, from following the sheep, that you should be prince over my people Israel. And I have been with you wherever you went and have cut off all your enemies from before you. And I will make for you a great name, like the name of the great ones of the earth…When your days are fulfilled and you lie down with your fathers, I will raise up your offspring after you, who shall come from your body, and I will establish his kingdom. He shall build a house for my name, and I will establish the throne of his kingdom forever. I will be to him a father…my steadfast love will not depart from him…and your house and your kingdom shall be made sure forever before me. Your throne shall be established forever."

Even though David brings up the Ark to Jerusalem, he will not allowed by God to build the Temple. An additional reason is tied to God's intent for His Temple, namely, it is to be a House of Peace. David, while serving the Lord faithfully; subduing and conquering many enemies – has a lot of the blood of the enemies of the Lord on his hands. The above passage is a Covenant the Lord establishes with David, in which He states, a son of David will be the one to build the Temple. How would David react and respond to these words? His heart had been set on building the permanent dwelling for The Ark - how would he handle this disappointment? Would he be overwhelmed with discourage-ment? Would he go ahead with his own personal plans? What will he do?

There is a record of David's response to this word from the Lord. It appears in I Chronicles 29 (Selected):

Verses 1-3: Personal Provision

"And David the king said to all the assembly, Solomon my son, whom alone God has chosen, is young and inexperienced, and the work is great, for the palace will not be for man but for the Lord God. So I have provided for the house of my God, so far as I was able, the gold for the things of gold, the silver for the things of silver, and the bronze for the things of bronze, the iron for the things of iron, and wood for the things of wood, besides great quantities of onyx and stones for setting, antimony, colored stones, all sorts of precious stones and marble. Moreover, in addition to all that I have provided for the holy house, I have a treasure of my own of gold and silver, and because of my devotion to the house of my God I give it to the house of my God…"

In verses 4-9, the rest of the people respond in kind and a great amount of treasure is amassed for the building of a permanent dwelling for the Lord in the midst of His people.

Verses 10-19: Personal Prayer

"Therefore David blessed the Lord in the presence of all the assembly. And David said: Blessed are you, O Lord, the God of Israel our father, forever and ever. Yours, O LORD, is the greatness and the power and the glory and the victory and the majesty, for all that is in the heavens and in the earth is yours. Yours is the kingdom, O Lord, and you are exalted as head above all. Both riches and honor come from you, and you rule over all. In your hand are power and might, and in your hand it is to make great and to give strength to all. And now we thank you, our God, and praise your glorious name. But who am I, and what is my people, that we should be able thus to offer willingly? For all things come from you, and of your own have we given you…O Lord our God, all this abundance that we have provided for building you a house for your holy name comes from your hand and is all your own. I know, my God, that you test the heart and have pleasure in uprightness. In the uprightness of my heart I have freely offered all these things, and now I have seen your people, who are present here, offering freely and joyously to you. O Lord…keep forever such purposes and thoughts in the hearts of your people, and direct their hearts toward you. Grant to Solomon my son a whole heart that he may keep your commandments, your testimonies, and your statutes, performing all, and that he may build the palace for which I have made provision."

Verses 20-25: Personal Proclamation

"Then David said to all the assembly, Bless the Lord your God. And all the assembly blessed the Lord, the God of their fathers, and bowed their heads and paid homage to the Lord and to the king. And they offered sacrifices to the Lord…with their drink offerings, and sacrifices in abundance for all Israel. And they ate and drank before the Lord on that day with great gladness. And they made Solomon the son of David kingThen Solomon sat on the throne of the Lord as king in place of David his father. And he prospered, and all Israel obeyed him…And the Lord made Solomon very great in the sight of all Israel and bestowed on him such royal majesty as had not been on any king before him in Israel."

Years pass and the Temple is being constructed. Later on, a unique moment occurs at the Dedication of Solomon's Temple. It is recorded in I Kings 8:6-11 – "…the priests brought the ark of the covenant of the Lord to its place in the inner sanctuary of the house, in the Most Holy Place, underneath the wings of the cherubim…There was nothing in the ark except the two tablets of stone that Moses put there at Horeb, where the Lord made a covenant with the people of Israel, when they came out of the land of Egypt. And when the priests came out of the Holy Place, a cloud filled the house of the Lord, so that the priests could not stand to minister because of the cloud, for the glory of the Lord filled the house of the Lord." Just think – as the people gather for this special event, and as they observe this magnificent structure – The Temple – as they stand in awe – they have a renewed oppor-tunity –

- Approaching The Temple and Being Fully Aware of The Glory of God At and In That Place
- The Reminder That God was once again Dwelling In The Midst of His People – As He Had Promised

- The Joy that Should Flow from Each Heart because of God's Presence, Protection and Provision.

Oh, The Glory Of His Presence!

Will the people be more seriously committed to the Lord and His purposes than they were before? Will they be more careful in observing God's directives to them? Will they be willingly obedient and disciplined in life and practice? Will they reverence and honor the Lord as He desires them to do? Will they remember The Creator - - - The Sabbath Day to keep it Holy - - - The Decalogue and the precepts of God - - - The reason for The Passover...? Will they Remember?

Regardless of the personal resolutions and intentions, the reality is that one will become lax and lenient in terms of ones spiritual

Disciplines. All Too Often - - -

- It is too easy to become routine with the things of God
- It is to easy to become matter-of-fact
- It is to easy to ignore the obvious –
- Being Silent When One Should Speak Up
- Being Accommodating When One Should Be More Exacting
- Relaxing Standards and Disregarding The Moral Compass
- It Becomes too easy to be Complacent
- It leads to one being De-Sensitized (seared conscience)
- It Allows One To Not Notice What Is Taking Place

When this becomes a lifestyle and the accepted norm, then the Reality and Dramatic Picture of Ezekiel 10 can and will occur. The picture drawn is of the progressive steps as the Glory of God

Departs from the Temple and the midst of the people. The Steps And Stages Of God's Glory Departing Once Again - - -

Ezekiel10:4-5 - The Glory Of God Is Beginning To Move

Step 1: From The Holy of Holies to the Threshold – "the glory of the Lord went up from the cherub to the threshold of the house, and the house was filled with the cloud, and the court was filled with the brightness of the glory of the Lord. And the sound of the wings of the cherubim was heard as far as the outer court, like the voice of God Almighty when he speaks."

To any observer who had interest in The Temple, the sound of the Glory of the Lord stirring and moving would've been profound. No one seemed to notice or pay attention!

Ezekiel 10:18-19   The Glory of God Moves From Threshold to Entrance of the East Gate

Step 2: "…Then the glory of the Lord went out from the threshold of the house, and stood over the cherubim. And the cherubim lifted up their wings and mounted up from the earth before my eyes as they went out, with the wheels beside them. And they stood at the entrance of the east gate of the house of the Lord, and the glory of the God of Israel was over them."

If The Temple was the center of attention; if it was the determining factor in their life and lifestyle of the people; if they were focused on God in their midst – why were they figuratively blind and deaf to what was taking place? What had become of greater importance to them?

Ezekiel 11:22-23   The Glory Of God Moves From The City to the Mountain

Step 3: "...Then the cherubim lifted up their wings, with the wheels beside them, and the glory of the God of Israel was over them. And the glory of the Lord went up from the midst of the city and stood on the mountain that is on the east side of the city."

Each progressive step has moments of pause. The Lord was in no rush to leave His people. If only there was an Abraham to plead with the Lord to allow him time to see if he could find at least fifty righteous people in the land of Sodom (Genesis 18:23-33), maybe the Lord would delay His departure. But – there was no intercessor, no one to plead with The Lord.

The reason for God's action and His Glory Departing is given in Ezekiel 11:10-12

"You shall fall by the sword. I will judge you at the border of Israel, and you shall know that I am the Lord. This city shall not be your cauldron, nor shall you be the meat in the midst of it. I will judge you at the border of Israel, and you shall know that I am the Lord. For you have not walked in my statutes, nor obeyed my rules, but have acted according to the rules of the nations that are around you."

- God Is Observing All Our Deeds and Actions
- He Is Hearing All Of Our Words and Nuances

In The Midst of This Shifting of the Glory of God, promises are made by The Lord regarding Israel in Ezekiel 11:17-20 - - -

"Therefore say, Thus says the Lord God: I will gather you from the peoples and assemble you out of the countries where you have been scattered, and I will give you the land of Israel. And when they come there, they will remove from it all its detestable things and all its abominations. And I will give them one heart, and a new spirit I will put within them. I will remove the heart of stone from their flesh and give them a heart of flesh, that they may walk in my statutes and keep my rules and obey them. And they shall be my people, and I will be their God."

Ironically – and – Despite the Movement of The Glory of God –

- No one seems to be paying too much attention
- There is no lament on the part of the People
- There is no seeking for the Mercy of God
- There is no change in behavior or direction

And Finally – Suddenly – The Reality - A new Ichabod moment and experience. The Glory has departed. The Glory of the Lord Is Gone! The Prophet is brought to the people and he shares with them the vision from the Lord - Ezekiel 11:24-25.

"And the Spirit lifted me up and brought me in the vision by the Spirit of God into Chaldea, to the exiles. Then the vision that I had seen went up from me. And I told the exiles all the things that the Lord had shown me."

The people may have listened but even though the Prophets words had been spoken and heard, they were met with a shrug of indifference and disinterest.

- No apparent alarm on the part of the people
- No pleading with the Lord to remain with them
- Just – Continued Apathy and Indifference

R.C. Sproul wrote in his Online Devotional: Living In The Presence of God - August 16th, 2010 on the theme of Restoring Our Relationship.

"Unregenerate man is consistently described as being in a state of alienation and enmity. This is the condition that makes reconciliation necessary. Reconciliation is necessary only when a state of estrangement exists between two or more parties. Estrangement is the natural fallen state of our relationship to God. How are we enemies of God?

"Jonathan Edwards provides an insightful summary of the problem. He lists several points of tension between God and man:

1. By nature, we have a low esteem of God. We count Him unworthy of our love or fear.
2. We prefer to keep a distance from God. We have no natural inclination to seek His presence in prayer.
3. Our wills are opposed to the law of God. We are not loyal subjects of His sovereign rule.
4. We are enemies against God in our affections. Our souls have a seed of malice against God. We are quick to blaspheme and to rage against Him.
5. We are enemies in practice. We walk in a way that is contrary to Him.

"Examine your spiritual condition in light of Edwards's five points of tension between God and man."

What makes the difference for an individual life? It is a personal relationship with Jesus Christ. It is an important and active relationship where growth and maturity noticeably takes place.

Difference #1: Being Redeemed and Adopted - Galatians 4:4-5 "But when the fullness of time had come, God sent forth his Son, born of woman, born under the law, to redeem those who were under the law, so that we might receive adoption as sons."

Difference #2: No Longer A Stranger To The Covenant of Promise - Ephesians 2:12 "At that time you were without Christ, being aliens from the commonwealth of Israel and strangers from the covenants of promise, having no hope & without God in the world."

Difference #3: Being Reconciled and Being Saved - Romans 5:10 "For if when we were enemies we were reconciled to God through the death of His Son, much more, having been reconciled, we shall be saved by His life."

Difference #4: Being Cognizant of His Glory - John 1:14 "And the Word became flesh and dwelt among us, and we have seen his glory, glory as of the only Son from the Father, full of grace and truth."

Personal Study Questions - - -

What does the Glory of God mean to and for you? Explain!

Have you become matter-of-fact regarding the place, value and importance of the Glory of God for you?

What does the discussion regarding The Glory of God mean to you?

You don't understand it?

You've never experienced or observed it?

Are you cognizant of the Glory of God being present in the place where you regularly worship?

How would you describe and define it?

Would you say it is more or less constant?

Based upon John 1:14,

Have YOU Seen/Beheld His Glory?

Have YOU Come Under His Grace?

Are YOU Standing On and In His Truth?

May You Always Be Able To Echo: To God Be The Glory – Great Things He Has Done (Is Doing)!

Amen!

The Retaining of the Glory of His Presence

Homeless! Friendless! Unemployed! Directionless! Lonely! Lost! Can you imagine what it would be like to lose one's way and wanting to stay lost? Can you think of what it would be like to be afraid or ashamed for one to turn around and admit the error of wrong choices? Can you sense what it would be like to be in a strange place, with no acquaintances and no one reaching out to be a friend? Can you feel what it would be like to be in a foreign geographic area, unaccustomed to the customs and language of your new locale – and the locals looking at one with suspicion and disdain? How can one get turned around? How can one find the right way back?

- If this applied to spiritual matters, how would one answer:
- What if one forgets all that's involved in living in the presence of God?
- What if one gets focused on personal circumstances and decides, I have to take matters into my own hands; I have to determine my own fate; I have to make the determination for my life and future?
- What if one decides: I want to get away from it all -this isn't where I want to be; this isn't what I want to do?

The Bible contains instances of those who turned their backs on God and His will and headed in the wrong direction - - -

- Jacob and his deception. He had become so willful and full of himself that there was little room for anyone or anything else. He had even managed to squeeze God out of his life and had not missed the Glory of His Presence. Part of his wrestling with God was to return him to the

place where he focused on someone other than himself,
He had done that for far too long. Now the time had come
for him to connect once again with the Lord – "I will not
let you go unless you bless me!"

- Elijah and his fear of a woman's threat to see him dead.
His neglect to remember and retain the Glory of His Presence and power – until he heard God's whisper (see be-
low)..

- Jonah and his disdain for the people of Nineveh. Not
wanting to be where God wanted him to be – so God allowed him to sink to the greatest depths to get his attention and remind him there is a God who will not be
denied or ignored. He must return to a place where he can
bask in the Glory of His Presence once again.

- A son and his disrespect for parental authority, such as,
the Prodigal Son – Luke 15. This entire scene brought
shame not only to the Prodigal but also to the Father who
had to sell part of his estate to meet the son's request and
demands. It wasn't until the son wound up eating garbage
and slop that he would come to his senses – retracing his
steps and heading towards home.

- Onesimus and his determination to escape slavery. He had
not calculated that he would meet the Apostle Paul and
hear the Gospel. He also had not calculated returning to
his earthly master and back into being a slave. It
represents a need to surrender one's rights and will. In
doing so, one will be able to be in that place of God's
choosing – to be in God's will. When that is the case, one
is safe and secure, and can once again embrace the Glory
of His Presence in and for one's life and all one's situations.

Getting turned around is never easy especially when the choice of
direction, albeit the wrong direction, was the matter of one's
personal choosing. Dr. Henry Brandt , a Christian Psychologist of

several years ago, related an incident in his life that goes something like the following:

"He tells of leaving a Family Life Conference and heading home! He and his wife, Eva, had spent the night in an excellent Motel; they had dined together on a sumptuous breakfast; and were making their journey in a luxury automobile. Their destination was Detroit. Shortly after getting on the Interstate, "Eva says: Henry – you're going the wrong way. "Henry exclaimed: Eva - I've driven this way before and I know where I'm going…A little bit further Eva once again says: Henry, you ARE going the wrong way! Henry exclaims: Eva! I know this road and I know where I'm going! It IS the right way. In a few more miles, Henry sees a sign with an arrow pointing that they are actually headed toward Chicago.

"Henry shared: As a Christian Psychologist – I know how to assimilate data and information…

• I have counseled people how to deal with obvious errors…
• I have counseled people how to admit when one is wrong and to quickly work on correction…
• I have counseled people of the benefit of being humble and to admit when one has been wrong…
• I have counseled people that it is right to ask for forgiveness for the behavior displayed in asserting one IS right…

"However – Henry also shared that he drove past two additional Exits trying to figure out how to get turned around without admitting to his wife that (a) she had been right all along, and (b) they were in fact driving in the wrong direction."

The hope and expectation is for one to come to a point of reality that what is being done, and the direction one is headed is incorrect behavior and change of direction must occur.

There is an incident in I Kings 19:3-5 where a prophet of the Lord finds himself in a situation that he believes he alone must find a solution and bring about finality. What will he do? Where will he go? Has he sought any counsel? Has he asked for God's guidance and protection?

The text states: "Elijah was afraid and ran for his life. When he came to Beersheba in Judah, he left his servant there, while he himself went a day's journey into the desert. He came to a broom tree, sat down under it and prayed that he might die. I have had enough, Lord, he said. Take my life; I am no better than my ancestors. Then he lay down under the tree and fell asleep. He had allowed himself to succumb to fear, despair and depression. Elijah processed the wrong data - - -

- He allowed a threat by a wicked woman, Jezebel, to impact his thinking.
- He believed the threat.
- He chose to take a personal action without consulting the Lord in terms of His will.

He had forgotten the peril awaiting the one who takes the affairs and matters of his own life direction into his own hands.

Getting out of the will of God can be and will be disastrous.

- It allowed him to forget the power of God for and in his life.
- Fear, despair, and depression can impact one – and -
- It can cause one to come to a wrong conclusion.

- It can enable one to rationalize that the wrong direction is the only right direction to take.
- It will also enable one to become resolute in the decision reached and the conclusion drawn.

Elijah so desperately needed to call upon the Lord

To cast his Burden upon the Lord.

To cast all of his care upon Him.

Let's pause and ask ourselves:

- Do you ever find yourself in an impossible circumstance because of a decision you have made?
- Have you ever been at the place where you just wanted to escape and be alone – maybe even die?
- Have you faced a difficult challenge and ignored God – the One Who is your ever-present help?
- Anything religious or spiritual was the last thing on your mind?
- Can it Happen to You?   Yes!!!!

However, the Lord never gives up on or forgets one of His own.

- He would come and wrestle with Jacob until he yielded his will and behavior to God.
- He would allow Jonah to come to a point of desperation where he would cry out for God's help and deliverance.
- He would bring Onesimus into contact with Paul, who would persuade him to return to his master and serve him better than before his running away.
- He will seek Elijah out, provide for him and confront him directly.

Note the Lord's patience and care for Elijah in I Kings 19:11-15. Elijah will be reminded about the significance of the presence of the Lord.

"The LORD said, Go out and stand on the mountain in the presence of the Lord, for the Lord is about to pass by.

- Then a great and powerful wind tore the mountains apart and shattered the rocks before the Lord, but the Lord was not in the wind.
- After the wind there was an earthquake, but the Lord was not in the earthquake.
- After the earthquake came a fire, but the Lord was not in the fire.
- And after the fire came a gentle whisper.

"When Elijah heard it, he pulled his cloak over his face and went out and stood at the mouth of the cave. Then a voice said to him, What are you doing here, Elijah? He replied:

- I have been very zealous for the Lord God Almighty.
- The Israelites have rejected your covenant.
- They have broken down your altars, and
- They have put your prophets to death with the sword.
- I am the only one left, and now they are trying to kill me too.
- The Lord said to him, Go back the way you came."

What had Elijah allowed himself to forget? What happened to his memory of the power of God displayed on Mount Carmel? Do you suppose God is allowing this flight and hiding to bring Elijah to the place where he realizes he has failed to remember and retain the Glory of God's Presence in his mind, soul and life? Isn't that the real issue, not just for Elijah, but for all who purpose to walk with the Lord – beginning to look at self and forgetting to look at the Glory of His Presence?

Remaining silent before the Lord is oftentimes difficult. One is so full of his fears, doubts, problems, aloneness, complaints. Changing direction is never easy either. Admitting one is wrong and going in the wrong direction is difficult at best. Making the necessary adjustment can also be hard. To change the direction one is going will require (a) humility, (b) obedience and (c) willingness. Many times it is so difficult, especially when the trials and difficulties seem to be the greatest, to grasp that God is doing a special work in us. It is based upon His perfect will and plan for us. It is always motivated by his love for us. It includes one's understanding of Hebrews 12:4-10,

"In your struggle against sin, you have not yet resisted to the point of shedding your blood. And you have forgotten that word of encouragement that addresses you as sons: My son, do not make light of the Lord's discipline, and do not lose heart when he rebukes you, because the Lord disciplines those he loves, and he punishes everyone he accepts as a son. Endure hardship as discipline; God is treating you as sons. For what son is not disciplined by his father? If you are not disciplined…then you are illegitimate children and not true sons. Moreover, we have all had human fathers who disciplined us and we respected them for it. How much more should we submit to the Father of our spirits and live! Our fathers disciplined us for a little while as they thought best; but God disciplines us for our good, that we may share in his holiness." What is God's objective for His people? It is (a) "for our good, and (b) to bring one to the place where "we may share in His holiness."

The same challenge for Elijah exists for everyone in the process of redemption.   One's focus on redemption necessitates an understanding of what redemption means. Redemption is God's paying the ransom or price for sin Himself. Redemption is deliverance by the payment of a price. This Source of that redemption is expressed Ephesians 1:7, "In him we have redemption through his blood, the forgiveness of our trespasses, according to the riches of his grace." The Greek word translated "redemption" in Ephesians 1:7 is an intensified form of lutroo, which refers to paying a price to free someone from bondage.

During NT times, the Roman empire had approximately 20 million slaves, and the buying and selling of them was major business. If a person wanted to free a loved one or friend who was a slave, he would buy the slave for himself and then grant him freedom. He would testify to that deliverance by a written certificate. Lutroo was used to designate such a transaction.

One must also understand what salvation means and includes:

Justification—the sinner stands before God accused, but is declared righteous because of his position in Christ (Romans 8:33).

Forgiveness--the sinner stands before God as a debtor, but his obligation brought by sin is canceled (Ephesians 1:7).

Adoption--the sinner stands before God as a stranger, but is made a son (Ephesians 1:5).

Reconciliation--the sinner stands before God as an enemy, but is made a friend (2 Corinthians 5:18-20).

Redemption--the sinner stands before God as a slave, but receives freedom (Romans 6:18:22).

If one is to retain the Glory of His Presence, there will need to be an additional understanding in terms of how one gains the benefit of salvation and purposeful fellowship with God. It will always include Repentance. The American Heritage Dictionary Defines Repentance as:

1. To feel remorse, contrition, or self-reproach for what one has done or failed to do; be contrite.

2. To feel such regret for past conduct as to change one's mind regarding it

3. To make a change for the better as a result of remorse or contrition for one's sins.

Biblically, repentance includes an additional definition. When "metanoia" is used in the New Testament, it always speaks of a change of purpose, and specifically a turning from sin. Repentance is not merely being ashamed or sorry over sin. It is also a redirection of the human will: "a purposeful decision to forsake all unrighteousness and pursue righteousness instead."

In actuality, Elijah needed to repent - to change his mind, will, purpose and direction. This change and journey will be difficult for Elijah. He will have to deal with his self-pity; his apprehension and reluctance; his personal pride – and – he will have to return to the place where everyone knew why and when he fled. One can only surmise and suppose that the return journey was slower and more prolonged than when he left/fled. However, each step he would take will bring him closer to full and complete repentance, that is, getting back to the place where God had wanted him all along.

Repentance is a key thrust in the New Testament.

- John the Baptist came preaching repentance.
- Jesus Christ preached and taught about repentance

- The apostles primary message was:
- Repent…
- Be converted…
- Be baptized
- Revelation 2 and 3 – as Jesus walks in the midst of the churches, His declaration to them included:
- I know all about you
- You who have ears to hear – hear what the spirit is saying to you - - -
- Remember, repent and return.

In a devotional, Dr. R.C. Sproul wrote about: "In The Presence of God - Comprehending the Course of History."

"What is striking in this history is the manifest hand of providence in the work of redemption. God is a God of long-range planning. He does not succumb to the all-too-human tendency toward immediate gratification and short-term goals. God sees the end from the beginning and rules the course of history, moving it inexorably toward its appointed destiny. In the affairs of the life of Abraham, God was providentially directing history toward David's kingship and far beyond to the kingship of Christ.

The genealogies show that the first advent of Christ was not an after-thought in God's mind, a sudden quick-fix remedy for a world run amok. Rather, it displays a marvelous drama of redemption that God ordained before the foundation of the world and gradually but surely brought to pass in the footnotes of history. All who rejoice in the first advent are comforted by the certainty of the promised second advent. We, as twenty-first-century Christians, live in an interim period—the time between two advents that define, condition, and redeem the meaning of our lives."

There are many distractions in the world that could easily prevent one from Retaining the Glory of God's Presence as the priority for one's life. Human discipline has seemed to wane and Spiritual discipline is not lagging too far behind. There is an inordinate tolerance of the distracting stuff in both the world and church. Some of it seems so right and so good, and more and more of it is embraced and squeezed into an already crowded life. The end result is going through the right motions but not for the correct reason. Within that religious exercise, one must always be cognizant of this thought: Will this bring one into closer relationship with the Lord where the Glory of His Presence is retained and championed.

The question remains: Do you need to repent? Are you ready to commit yourself to Christ where there will be (a) a change of your mind, (b) a change of your will, and (c) a change of your purpose and direction?

A much broader question is: Do we need to repent? Do we need to get back to the place where God wants us to be? Think about it. More importantly, remember, repent, return - now!!

The words of Dr. Henry Brandt are so appropriate: "If I go to Heaven before you, I would like to be holding the tape when you finish the race God has given you to run." We need to run that race with patience and reach that finish line.

Personal Study Questions - - -

Have you ever lost your way but were too proud to retrace your steps and head back to where you were supposed to be – maybe even returning home?

Have you ever headed off in a direction of your choosing – just wanting to get away from it all – and everyone? Why?

Have you tried to find a "cave" where you can either sulk or meditate? Did you listen for God's whisper?

Have you made certain determinations and decisions that you knew you should not have made – but – believing you were a free moral agent – you made them anyway?

Is it your personal desire to retain the Glory of His Presence in your daily life? How do you propose to do it?

In 1825, Joseph Bowring penned the very meaningful words to the Hymn - - -

> In the cross of Christ I glory,
> Towering o'er the wrecks of time;
> All the light of sacred story
> Gathers round its head sublime.
>
> When the woes of life o'ertake me,
> Hopes deceive, and fears annoy,
> Never shall the cross forsake me,
> Lo! it glows with peace and joy.

May you always cling to that cross and the Savior who died on it for you, basking in the Glory of His Presence.

The Ultimate Glory of His Presence

As Jesus prepared His disciples for His death and ascension, He said (John 14:1-3), "Let not your hearts be troubled. Believe in God; believe also in me. In my Father's house are many rooms. If it were not so, would I have told you that I go to prepare a place for you? And if I go and prepare a place for you, I will come again and will take you to myself, that where I am you may be also." The new Living Translation is: "Don't be troubled. You trust God, now trust in me. There are many rooms in my Father's home, and I am going to prepare a place for you. If this were not so, I would tell you plainly. When everything is ready, I will come and get you, so that you will always be with me where I am." Jesus is telling His disciples about a place called Heaven. At the very least, heaven is:

1.   A Particular Place. Notice the references to "you" in the text. Jesus has "you" on His mind.

2.   A Prepared Place. Jesus has obligated Himself to "go and prepare a place for you." It is unique and special because He is the Chief Architect for this place called Heaven.

3.   A Promised Place. "I will come again and will take you to myself, that where I am you may be also."

It is very unique in that no one deserves to go there; no one can earn his way there; and no one can purchase a place there.

What an interesting phrase Jesus employs – "when everything is ready" – one leaves this planet and enters into eternity to be in the Glory of the Presence of the Triune God forever! A major consideration is whether or not one is ready to exit this planet and enter into eternity. In that regard, an older Hymn written by P.P. Bliss includes this stanza:

> Almost persuaded now to believe;
> Almost persuaded Christ to receive;
> Seems now some soul to say, Go, Spirit, go Thy way,
> Some more convenient day On Thee I'll call.

The words of the hymn "Almost Persuaded" contain the excuses and rationale of many who delay any concern for their soul and eternity. A Campus Minister would often use this appeal as he presented the Gospel – "Eternity is a long time to spend in the wrong place." It is a shame and tragedy that one would delay to the "some more convenient day" rather than to choose now the certainty, hope and assurance that allows one to know that "to be absent from the body" will mean that one is "present with the Lord.

How different are the words in the Hymn written in 1871 from the words of a contemporary anthem written by Don Wyrtzen, in 1971, words that are very compelling and definitive. The Anthem is entitled: Finally Home.

> When engulfed by the terror of the tempestuous sea,
> Unknown waves before you roll;
> At the end of doubt and peril is eternity,
> Though fear and conflict seize your soul.

> When surrounded by the blackness of the darkest night,
> O how lonely death can be;
> At the end of this long tunnel is a shining light,
> For death is swallowed up in victory!
> Refrain:
> But just think - -
> Of stepping on shore – And finding it Heaven!

Of touching a hand – And finding it God's!
Of breathing new air – And finding it celestial!
Of waking up in glory – And finding it home!

There are meaningful examples of those who persevered amid trying circumstances. They were sustained by their hope. One of these examples is Job. In the midst of his considerable suffering and losses, he was able to look beyond his immediate circumstances. He exclaims from the depths of his soul – Job 19:23-27, "Oh that my words were written! Oh that they were inscribed in a book! Oh that with an iron pen and lead they were engraved in the rock forever! For I know that my Redeemer lives, and at the last he will stand upon the earth. And after my skin has been thus destroyed, yet in my flesh I shall see God, whom I shall see for myself, and my eyes shall behold, and not another. My heart faints within me!" It's his comfort as he thinks about what God's plan and purpose is for his life, that if he dies, he'll know fully and completely what it means to be:

- Stepping on shore – and finding it Heaven!
- Of touching a hand – and finding it God's!
- Of breathing new air – and finding it celestial!
- Of waking up in glory – and finding it home!

In much the same manner, the Apostle Paul echoed similarly his sense of death and eternity. He describes the place called heaven in these excerpts taken from II Corinthians 5:1-10, "…we know that if the tent that is our earthly home is destroyed, we have a building from God, a house not made with hands, eternal in the heavens. For in this tent we groan, longing to put on our heavenly dwelling…For while we are still in this tent, we groan, being burdened–not that we would be unclothed, but that we would be further clothed, so that what is mortal may be swallowed up by life. He who has prepared us for this very thing is God, who has given us the Spirit as a guarantee…We know that while we are at home in the body we are away from the Lord, for we walk by faith, not by sight…we would rather be away from the body and at home with the Lord. So whether we are at home or away, we make it our aim to please him." This is the blessed hope of the child of God – when life is ended, he/she will be safe in the arms of Jesus forever. For him, it meant nothing more nor anything less than – whether through death, or by the second coming of Jesus Christ – presence with the Lord is ones hope and assurance. It bears out the words of hope and assurance in the Anthem - - -

- Of stepping on shore – and finding it Heaven!
- Of touching a hand – and finding it God's!
- Of breathing new air – and finding it celestial!
- Of waking up in glory – and finding it home!

The Apostle Paul longed for the heavenly home and wrestled within himself regarding this matter. He shared in Philippians 1:21-28 his inner thoughts and rationale in these words, "For to me to live is Christ, and to die is gain. If I am to live in the flesh, that means fruitful labor for me. Yet which I shall choose I cannot tell. I am hard pressed between the two. My desire is to depart and be with Christ, for that is far better. But to remain in the flesh is more necessary on your account. Convinced of this, I know that I will remain and continue with you all, for your progress and joy in the faith, so that in me you may have ample cause to glory in Christ Jesus, because of my coming to you again. Only let your manner of life be worthy of the gospel of Christ, so that whether I come and see you or am absent, I may hear of you that you are standing firm in one spirit, with one mind striving side by side for the faith of the gospel, and not frightened in anything by your opponents…" The key to what he is sharing is in these words: "I am hard pressed between the two. My desire is to depart and be with Christ, for that is far better. But to remain in the flesh is more necessary on your account." The NLT paraphrases verses 23-24, "I'm torn between two desires: Sometimes I want to live, and sometimes I long to go and be with Christ. That would be far better for me, but it is better for you that I live…"

Two servants of the Lord had a special opportunity of looking into Heaven by way of a vision and writing about what they had seen. The first is in Isaiah 6:1-7, "In the year that King Uzziah died I saw the Lord sitting upon a throne, high and lifted up; and the train of his robe filled the temple. Above him stood the seraphim. Each had six wings: with two he covered his face, and with two he covered his feet, and with two he flew. And one called to another and said: Holy, holy, holy is the Lord of hosts; the whole earth is full of his glory! And the foundations of the thresholds shook at the voice of him who called, and the house was filled with smoke. And I said: Woe is me! For I am lost; for I am a man of unclean lips, and I dwell in the midst of a people of unclean lips; for my eyes have seen the King, the Lord of hosts! Then one of the seraphim flew to me, having in his hand a burning coal that he had taken with tongs from the altar. And he touched my mouth and said: Behold, this has touched your lips; your guilt is taken away, and your sin atoned for." This will result in Isaiah's willingness to carry God's Word and message to whomever and wherever. It is borne out in his words, "Here am I, send me!" It is an unconditional commitment to be God's representative to any place or situation. Once one has been in the Presence of the Lord, ones life should be markedly and dramatically different. It's no longer "I" but "Christ" who is now seen. This thought was written in a Hymn in 1891. It is expressed well in these stanzas:

> Not I, but Christ, be honored, loved, exalted;
> Not I, but Christ, be seen be known, be heard;
> Not I, but Christ, in every look and action,
> Not I, but Christ, in every thought and word.
> Christ, only Christ! No idle words e'er falling,
> Christ, only Christ; no needless bustling sound;

Christ, only Christ; no self important bearing;
Christ, only Christ; no trace of "I" be found.

The Second servant of the Lord who had a special opportunity of
looking into Heaven by way of a vision and writing about it was
the Apostle John. The Book of Revelation is a record of what he
saw and was directed to write. The Prologue to the Book –
Revelation 1:1-3 – states: "The revelation of Jesus Christ, which
God gave him to show to his servants the things that must soon
take place. He made it known by sending his angel to his servant
John, who bore witness to the word of God and to the testimony
of Jesus Christ, even to all that he saw. Blessed is the one who
reads aloud the words of this prophecy, and blessed are those who
hear, and who keep what is written in it, for the time is near."

The first thing John saw when he looked into Heaven is written in
Revelation 4. Some selected excerpts are: "After this I looked,
and behold, a door standing open in heaven! And the first voice,
which I had heard speaking to me like a trumpet, said, Come up
here, and I will show you what must take place after this. At once
I was in the Spirit, and behold, a throne stood in heaven, with one
seated on the throne…Around the throne were twenty-four
thrones, and seated on the thrones were twenty-four elders,
clothed in white garments, with golden crowns on their
heads…And around the throne, on each side of the throne, are
four living creatures…And the four living creatures…day and
night they never cease to say, Holy, holy, holy, is the Lord God
Almighty, who was and is and is to come! And whenever the
living creatures give glory and honor and thanks to him who is
seated on the throne, who lives forever and ever, the twenty-four
elders fall down before him who is seated on the throne and
worship him who lives forever and ever. They cast their crowns
before the throne, saying, Worthy are you, our Lord and God, to
receive glory and honor and power, for you created all things, and
by your will they existed and were created." He saw a scene of

worship, glory and praise before the throne of Jesus – "Worthy are You, our Lord and God…"

What a thrilling vision and journey John had and shares. As he nears the conclusion of what he will write, in Revelation 21:1-9 he shares this description: "…I saw a new heaven and a new earth, for the first heaven and the first earth had passed away, and the sea was no more. And I saw the holy city, new Jerusalem, coming down out of heaven from God, prepared as a bride adorned for her husband. And I heard a loud voice from the throne saying, Behold, the dwelling place of God is with man. He will dwell with them, and they will be his people, and God himself will be with them as their God. He will wipe away every tear from their eyes, and death shall be no more, neither shall there be mourning, nor crying, nor pain anymore, for the former things have passed away. And he who was seated on the throne said, Behold, I am making all things new. Also he said, Write this down, for these words are trustworthy and true. And he said to me, It is done! I am the Alpha and the Omega, the beginning and the end. To the thirsty I will give from the spring of the water of life without payment. The one who conquers will have this heritage, and I will be his God and he will be my son. But as for the cowardly, the faithless, the detestable, as for murderers, the sexually immoral, sorcerers, idolaters, and all liars, their portion will be in the lake that burns with fire and sulfur, which is the second death."

In reading the words spoken, "…he who was seated on the throne said, Behold, I am making all things new…" reminds one of the words in II Corinthians 5:11-19 (selected), "Therefore, knowing the fear of the Lord, we persuade others… For the love of Christ controls us, because we have concluded this: that one has died for all, therefore all have died – he died for all, that those who live might no longer live for themselves but for him who for their sake died and was raised…Therefore, if anyone is in Christ, he is a new creation. The old has passed away; behold, the new has come…" Yes! The time for the new has arrived – a new heaven and a new earth; a new dwelling place and a new environment; a new reality and a new experience – in the Ultimate Glory of His Presence forever.

John, in his jubilation, writes in Revelation 22:12-21 (selected),

"Behold, I am coming soon, bringing my recompense with me, to repay everyone for what he has done. I am the Alpha and the Omega, the first and the last, the beginning and the end. Blessed are those who wash their robes, so that they may have the right to the tree of life and that they may enter the city by the gates… I, Jesus, have sent my angel to testify to you about these things for the churches…The Spirit and the Bride say, Come. And let the one who hears say, Come. And let the one who is thirsty come; let the one who desires take the water of life without price…He who testifies to these things says, Surely I am coming soon. Amen. Come, Lord Jesus! The grace of the Lord Jesus be with all. Amen."

In 1900, Charles H. Gabriel wrote the words and music to a grand testimony of hope and expectation:

> When all my labors and trials are o'er,
> And I am safe on that beautiful shore,
> Just to be near the dear Lord I adore,
> Will through the ages be glory for me.
> When, by the gift of His infinite grace,
> I am accorded in Heaven a place,
> Just to be there and to look on His face,
> Will through the ages be glory for me.
>
> Friends will be there I have loved long ago;
> Joy like a river around me will flow;

Yet just a smile from my Savior, I know,
Will through the ages be glory for me.
Refrain
O that will be glory for me,
Glory for me, glory for me,
When by His grace I shall look on His face,
That will be glory, be glory for me.

In John 14, when Jesus shared with His followers where He was going and what He would be doing, He also shared with them words about the legacy and gift He has arranged for them. It is contained in verse 27, "Peace I leave with you; my peace I give to you. Not as the world gives do I give to you. Let not your hearts be troubled, neither let them be afraid." It is a legacy and gift of His perfect peace. It can only be enjoyed and appreciated when one reaches out by faith and receives it.

Personal Study Questions - - -

Do you have a troubled or anxious heart as you consider the future and all of its unknowns? Why? On what basis?

Are you an "Almost Persuaded" person in terms of eternity or a Convinced and Committed person? Explain!

If you died today and stood in the presence of God, and He said: Why should I let you into My Heaven, what would your answer be? Explain your answer.

Do you know with certainty that your sins have been forgiven and that you are heaven-bound? What Scriptures have convinced you of that hope and truth? (A Helpful Hint: Read – I John 5:9-15, and highlight every key word and/or phrase in the text).

Are you ready and eager to enter into The Ultimate Glory of His Presence?

The Aaronic Benediction – Numbers 6:24-26

"The Lord bless you and keep you;
The Lord make His face shine upon you,
And be gracious to you;
The Lord lift up His countenance upon you,
And give you peace."

Concluding Thoughts

Many excellent books have been written on Holiness, Godliness and Righteousness. The attempt of this offering is that the child of God will sense the need of and have the desire for a greater awareness of the Glory of the Lord's Presence in a daily walk and relationship with Him.

A Sunday School Teacher wrote in a Bible that was given as a gift these words:

"This Book will keep you from the devil –
The devil will try to keep you from This Book."
That is the key understanding from two verses in Psalm 119 –
I have stored up your word in my heart,
that I might not sin against you.
Your word is a lamp to my feet
and a light to my path.

May you embrace as the commitment and guideline for your life the words of Psalm 19:8-14 - - -

The precepts of the Lord are right, rejoicing the heart; the commandment of the Lord is pure, enlightening the eyes; the fear of the Lord is clean, enduring forever; the rules of the Lord are true, and righteous altogether. More to be desired are they than gold, even much fine gold; sweeter also than honey and drippings of the honeycomb. Moreover, by them is your servant warned; in keeping them there is great reward. Who can discern his errors? Declare me innocent from hidden faults. Keep back your servant also from presumptuous sins; let them not have dominion over me! Then I shall be blameless, and innocent of great transgression. Let the words of my mouth and the meditation of my heart be acceptable in your sight, O Lord, my rock and my redeemer."

A prayer for you is from III John 2-4 - - -

"Beloved, I pray that all may go well with you and that you may be in good health, as it goes well with your soul. For I rejoiced greatly when the brothers came and testified to your truth, as indeed you are walking in the truth. I have no greater joy than to hear that my children are walking in the truth."

May God bless you and keep you as you commit yourself more and more to both know and walk in the Glory of His Presence,

About the Author

James Perry was born and reared in Brooklyn, NY and lived there for the first twenty years of his life. In the providence of God, he went to work at Lakeside Bible Conference in Carmel, NY and roomed in a two-man cabin with one who was the President of the Student Body of Columbia Bible College in Columbia, SC. This roommate was persistent throughout the summer as he asked him whether or not he knew God's purpose and will for his life.

At the end of the summer, he rode to Columbia, SC with some friends who had previously enrolled in Columbia Bible College, his thought being that he would hitch-hike back home. The Lord had other plans for his life and he was allowed to enroll and begin studying for the ministry there from 1954-57. He completed his College work at Covenant College, now located at Lookout Mountain, GA and went on to Covenant Theological Seminary in St. Louis, MO and completed that training in 1964.

Part of the Lord's plan for his life was to bring a young woman into his life during his freshman year. They were united in marriage in 1956 and have been partners in ministry from that point of time onward. The Lord has given him and his wife, Peggy, four children, fourteen grandchildren, and four great-grandchildren.

He has served as Pastor for more than forty-six years in churches from New Jersey to Colorado to Alabama - with some in-between - and have had great joy in doing so.

It is his hope and prayer that the lessons learned over many years will be helpful and instructive for you.